1995

Measuring Up

Robert Rothman

Measuring Up

Standards, Assessment, and School Reform

Jossey-Bass Publishers • San Francisco

Substantial discounts on bulk quantities of Jossey-Bass books are available to corporations, professional associations, and other organizations. For details and discount information, contact the special sales department at Jossey-Bass Inc., Publishers. (415) 433-1740; Fax (800) 605-2665.

For sales outside the United States, please contact your local Paramount Publishing International Office.

TCF Manufactured in the United States of America on Lyons Falls Pathfinder Tradebook. This paper is acid-free and 100 percent totally chlorine-free.

Library of Congress Cataloging-in-Publication Data

Rothman, Robert, date.
    Tests of significance : standards, assessment, and school reform / Robert Rothman.—1 ed.
        p.   cm.—(The Jossey-Bass education series)
    Includes bibliographical references (p.) and index.
    ISBN 0-7879-0055-9 (alk. paper)
    1. Achievement tests—United States—Evaluation. 2. Educational evaluation—United States. I. Title. II. Series.
  LB3060. 3. R68 1995
  371.2'64—dc20   94-43300
                                        CIP

FIRST EDITION
HB Printing 10 9 8 7 6 5 4 3 2 1   Code 9518

The Jossey-Bass Education Series

Contents

Preface

One of the most abused terms in discussions about education over the past few years is *revolution*. Almost any change in practice or policy, it seems, from the introduction of computers to school-based management, is described as *revolutionary*. While many such reforms lead to fundamental change, which is the dictionary definition of a revolution, that characterization in most cases exaggerates the true nature of the innovation.

Of all the changes that have acquired that distinction, though, the reform in the way schools think about student testing comes perhaps the closest to earning it. Unlike many of the other reforms, which transform only pieces of the system, however important, changes in testing go to the heart of the education enterprise: what students should know and be able to do. From the outset of schooling in America, educators have turned to tests as a way of determining whether schools have succeeded or not in their essential mission.

Moreover, because of their centrality in schooling, tests affect so many other aspects of the endeavor. While it may be true that changes in tests cannot by themselves change schools, it is also true that it is nearly impossible to change *just* a test. Changes in curriculum, in instruction, in school organization, and in many other areas will surely follow.

In recent years, schools have been sweeping away traditional notions of how we know what students know. Rather than taking students out of the normal class setting, giving them questions, seeing if they answer correctly or not, and evaluating their performance in comparison with their peers, schools now are setting standards for what all students should know and be able to do and allowing them to demonstrate, by writing essays, solving mathematics problems, or analyzing historical documents, whether they have attained the standards.

In schools that have undertaken such changes, teachers and parents have a different view of what students know. No longer do students "know" math when they score in the seventy-fifth percentile on a math test; rather, students know math when they can demonstrate that they can apply math principles to solve a new problem and communicate their results. At the same time, teachers have found that they must change everything they do to help prepare students to do well on such assessments. Lecturing and assigning chapters from a textbook are not enough; teachers must enable students to take more responsibility for their own learning and ensure that they understand the content and skills.

More fundamentally, the shift in view about student assessment is turning the traditional notion of education itself on its head. For most of this century, we have defined education by what goes into the system—the number of teachers, library books, and courses we provided—and tests have indicated which students got more out of the system and which got less. The revamped system, by contrast, begins with outcomes—what students should leave school knowing and being able to do. The inputs are important only to the extent that they lead students to the desired outcomes. Such a transformation, if widely adopted, would be truly radical. It would change the definition of an educated student from one who went through school to one who could demonstrate valued knowledge and skills. Eventually, it could lead to a system in which children would be entitled to learn, not just entitled to access to learning. Thus those attempting to change the way we measure student performance are really trying to transform the entire education system.

But if this shift is indeed revolutionary, it is a revolution in progress. First, in many places educators at the forefront of change face fierce rearguard battles from parents and community members who consider the reforms misguided and potentially dangerous. These opponents rightly see the standards schools are setting for all students as a radical departure from the kind of schooling they knew as students, and they remain skeptical of such changes. This skepticism is deepest in places that consider their schools exemplary and see no need for change. Although the opposition has scuttled changes in a few sites, educators and public officials remain convinced that an educated workforce and an informed citizenry demand high levels of learning among all young people. They will continue to fight for the changes.

Second, educators and researchers are still wrestling with the problem of building new assessment instruments that are valid, reliable, and fair methods of measuring student performance. Although the problems with the existing tools are well documented, the reformed system demands a technology that is still under development.

Finally, no one has yet created an entire system that would ensure that all students can attain high standards for performance. If the designers of the new system truly believe that all young people can learn at high levels, they must ensure that all schools have the capacity to bring about that goal. This is an enormous task, particularly in the face of gaping inequalities between advantaged and disadvantaged youths.

Measuring Up examines the shift in thinking about testing by looking at how it came about and what the new methods look like in practice. It is intended to explain, primarily to a general audience and to professionals who have not been intimately involved in the reform movement, a movement that has been little heralded and even less understood, but one that has enormous potential for transforming schools.

First, let me state what the book is *not*. It is not a manual for teachers that explains how to create new standards and new methods of assessment. Nor is it an essay on the philosophy behind the new methods. Other books exist that serve those purposes. Rather, this book is a general overview, from the perspective of a journalist who has observed the movement over the past decade, that attempts to cut through a debate that has too often been characterized by misrepresentations and jargon.

We will begin in Chapter One by examining the 1993 school board election in Littleton, Colorado, which brought out in dramatic relief the issues surrounding the shift to a new way of measuring student performance. We will then look closely inside classrooms in Littleton and elsewhere to see what variations on the new system look like, reviewing examples of what the schools expect of students and talking to teachers and administrators about how the changes in testing have changed teaching and learning.

In Chapter Two, we will step back and begin to examine how schools got to this point. We will look briefly at the history of testing in American schooling to show how the traditional view of student performance became entrenched. We will focus in particular on the explosion of "high-stakes" testing in the past two decades, which has made tests increasingly important in the classroom.

Chapter Three will examine the problems that have arisen as a result of the growth in testing and the search for alternatives. We will see how limiting and potentially harmful to student learning the traditional view has become and look at how emerging ideas about how students learn are contributing to a new view of how we measure student performance.

Chapter Four will look at several states that are developing alternatives to traditional ways of knowing what students know. As important as the school-level tests are, state tests have increasingly shaped what goes on in the classroom by holding consequences for students and schools. But a number of states have employed new knowledge to redefine what students should know and be able to do. We will examine some of the pioneering state programs and look at examples of what they expect from students.

Chapter Five will examine the movement for some form of national standards and system of assessments. Although national standards have long been anathema in a country that prizes local control over education, the national debate over this subject has risen rapidly up the agenda and has changed the conversation about education policy.

Chapter Six will examine in detail the problems schools are encountering as they attempt to change the way they know what young people know. We will focus primarily on Pennsylvania as an example of the political hurdles advocates of the new methods face and on emerging research findings that underscore the technical difficulties inherent in developing assessment methods that are valid, reliable, and fair.

Chapter Seven will point out some of the hurdles that will remain even if the new system is put in place. Without some way of ensuring that all students have an opportunity to learn, the new methods will not enable all students to perform at high levels. Likewise, without changes in the way teachers are taught, students will not benefit from the changes. But any change must begin with the end: what we want students to know and be able to do. And such a step demands a new way of knowing what students can achieve.

A few words of explanation are in order. This book focuses on achievement testing in elementary and secondary schools. There are many other tests, of course—some in the schools, such as college entrance examinations, and others in the nonschool world, such as driver's tests and professional licensing exams. Many of these have been affected by the changes in the view of measuring performance that are moving through schools. But I have chosen to focus on achievement tests for two reasons. First, because of the central position such tests occupy in schools. Adults who have been out of school for some time might be surprised at how ubiquitous achievement tests have become. By one estimate, the 41 million schoolchildren in America take 127 million tests annually, with some taking as many as twelve a year. By contrast, about a million high school seniors take the Scholastic Aptitude Test each year. And with the growth in testing has come testing's increasing influence over teaching and learning. The current moves for reform are aimed in large part at harnessing the power of testing for positive ends.

The second reason for focusing on school achievement tests is that schools occupy a central position in American society. Except for television, elementary and secondary schooling—the "common school"—is the only experience everyone shares. Defining what everyone in school should know and be able to do, and developing ways to know what students know, will have an enormous impact on society. Some have argued that a higher level of student performance is essential if America is to compete in the global economy. There is disagreement over that and over whether the primary goal of schooling should be to prepare young people for the workforce. But in any case, there is no doubt that the current approach, which sets low expectations overall—and in particular for the most disadvantaged members of society—must change. In a small but growing number of places, it *is* changing. And these changes are beginning with a new way of measuring student performance.

Acknowledgments

This book would not have come about without the support of two extraordinary groups of people, to whom I owe an incalculable debt. The first is the National Center for Research on Evaluation, Standards, and Student Testing at the Graduate School of Education, University of California, Los Angeles, where I was privileged to spend a year as a visiting researcher and write the manuscript. I am grateful to Dean Ted Mitchell and Director Eva Baker for inviting me there and allowing me to be a quasi colleague during a tumultuous year (fires, earthquakes). I am also indebted to my colleagues at the center, who welcomed me and shared their expertise and reacted to my work.

I also owe tremendous gratitude to the editors and staff of *Education Week*. Editor Ron Wolk and Executive Editor Ginny Edwards granted me a leave of absence to move to Los Angeles and work on the book, and for that I cannot begin to thank them. But I also need to thank them and their colleagues for the many years I worked alongside them. I learned all I know about education and much of what I know about writing while at *Education Week*. By any standard, they achieve at high levels.

Many individuals also contributed their time and support to help me with the book. I want especially to thank Ken Turner and the staff at Mark Twain Elementary School, Tim Westerberg and the staff at Littleton High School, Karen Bachover, Dale Carlson, Bill Cisney, Steve Ferrara, Chester Finn, Joan Herman, Andy Plattner, Ed Reidy, Lauren Resnick, Sue Rigney, Bob Stein, and David Stevenson. Lesley Iura at Jossey-Bass deserves thanks for her support and encouragement.

Finally, I owe a special debt to my son, Aaron Rothman, who put up with my absence for a year while I wrote this book. As he begins his formal educational journey, I hope that the ideas described here help make that experience as fulfilling as it can be. It is to him I dedicate this book.

Los Angeles, California   Robert Rothman
January 1995

The Author

Robert Rothman is a nationally known writer on educational policy and practice. For eight years he was editor and writer for *Education Week*. In 1993 and 1994, he was a visiting researcher at the National Center for Research on Evaluation, Standards, and Student Testing at the Graduate School of Education, University of California, Los Angeles. He is currently a senior associate at the National Alliance for Restructuring Education.

A 1980 graduate of Yale University with a bachelor's degree in political science, Rothman has been a Washington reporter since 1981. He has covered major developments at the local, state, and national levels in curriculum, testing, and education research, among other topics, and has spoken at a number of national conferences on education issues. Rothman's 1991 special report on cognitive science in education, "Thinking About Thinking," written with Debra Viadero, won the National Psychology Award for Excellence in Newspaper Writing from the American Psychological Association.

Prior to joining the staff of *Education Week*, Rothman was a reporter for the *Congressional Quarterly Weekly Report*. He has also written for a number of national publications and has contributed chapters to three books.

Measuring Up

Chapter One

A Clash of Visions

The 1993 school board election in Littleton, Colorado, was, by all accounts, the most bruising in memory. Articles and letters filled the local newspapers for weeks. Representatives of national organizations and newspaper reporters from around the country flocked to the Denver suburb to observe the proceedings. Residents jammed candidate forums. The nine candidates who vied for three contested seats spent unprecedented sums for advertisements, leaflets, and yard signs. And the rhetoric grew increasingly heated, with one group of candidates accusing the schools of foisting a misguided program on students that would harm them educationally, while their opponents accused the challengers of attempting to turn the clock back to a nonexistent past. The temperature rose a couple of degrees when People for the American Way, a national civil liberties group, distributed a questionnaire that sought to ascertain whether the schools' critics were "stealth" candidates for the religious right, a charge the candidates vehemently denied.

The campaign attracted extraordinary interest in the community. In the end, over 40 percent of the town's 58,700 voters cast ballots—ten times the turnout in the previous school board race.

The intensity of interest in the election matched the stakes involved. Schools in Littleton had embarked on a major reform effort that had thrust the suburban school district into the forefront of the national education-reform controversy. That reform was at stake in the election: incumbents on the school board and two other candidates pledged to uphold the reforms, while three other candidates vowed to kill the changes. And in a result that proved

1

even more astonishing than the contest itself, the anti-reform slate pulled off a major upset. By a two-to-one margin, voters elected the three critics of the reform effort to the three contested seats, giving them a majority on the five-member board. And the new majority quickly made good on their campaign promises. In their first months in office, they scrapped the reform program in the high schools and bought out the contract of the superintendent of schools.

What made this Littleton election so volatile? After all, school board elections in Littleton, like those in most places, are usually sleepy affairs that attract few candidates or voters other than school employees or parents with children in schools. Rarely do the elections result in major shifts in education policy.

But the 1993 Littleton election was different. In part, the intense interest in the race reflected a change in election law. That year, Littleton and several other Colorado communities experimented with a new form of balloting that enabled voters to mail in their ballots rather than troop down to the polls to cast them. The new system had the effect of making voting much more convenient and attracting the attention of large numbers of voters who might not otherwise have taken the trouble. In a community where about three-fourths of the voters do not have children in schools, this added interest made a difference in the outcome.

But more important than the procedural change was the substance of the contest. The election debate cut to the heart of schooling: What should students know and be able to do? And how should we determine whether they have attained such knowledge and skills? Few schools manage to ask those questions, much less make them the focus of a school board election. Yet not only did the Littleton schools ask them, in the years prior to the election, they answered them in a new way—a way that offers the potential of bringing about dramatic changes in American education. But as the election results show, these changes remain controversial.

Standards and Assessments in Littleton

The Littleton schools attempted, in the reform effort that was the cause of the controversy, to increase expectations for learning for all students and to develop new assessments to measure their learning. This is not to say the district did not already have high standards for its students. In many respects, Littleton students, like those in other affluent suburbs, were among the best performers in the country, and the town took great pride in the quality of its schools. Nearly all students graduated from high school, and the vast majority of the graduates went on to four-year colleges and universities, many to highly selective institutions. Students scored well above national averages on standardized tests.

But beginning in the late 1980s, when the school board authorized each school to restructure itself, administrators and teachers agreed that the system that had served Littleton well would no longer suffice. Scoring well above national averages means little if the averages are low. In addition, educators became convinced that the rapidly changing economy and the increasingly complex world demanded much higher levels of performance among all students. In the twenty-first century, they reasoned, all young people would have to be able to use their knowledge to solve problems, analyze information, and communicate clearly. But traditional tests not only failed to provide information on those abilities, they discouraged schools from tapping them by placing a premium on the quick recall of facts. Moreover, while the traditional system allowed some to excel, it also permitted many students simply to get by.

As Monte C. Moses, the former principal of Mark Twain Elementary School in Littleton, puts it:

> [O]ur [test] scores didn't mean as much when we looked at national statistics and statistics from our own building that showed that kids weren't very good problem solvers. Those scores also didn't mean much when we sat together at meetings and bemoaned the fact that

the character and civility of children seemed to be eroding, and that when you sat down with children individually and asked them to tell you something they had accomplished that they were proud of, they weren't able to answer.

So although the achievement score variable was in place, we also had hard data on those other elements that said students really weren't doing that well. Students were learning things that they weren't retaining.[1]

In place of the traditional practice, the Littleton schools proposed a wholly new system. Although each school went about its reforms in its own way, the schools generally headed toward the same goal: (1) setting standards that called for all students to demonstrate the ability to reason, solve problems, and communicate and (2) developing new assessments to measure such abilities by having students generate questions, work in groups to discuss problems, gather information independently and collectively, and write essays and make oral presentations on their own explaining their reasoning. But the teachers and administrators who created the new systems did not end there. They made the standards and assessments the centerpiece of a school restructuring effort. Using the standards for student performance as a goal, they redesigned their organizational structures and instructional practices to attain that goal. And to the teachers and to many parents whose children attended the schools, the new efforts were the way to go.

But to another group of parents—and, it turned out, to many residents without children in the schools—the new systems were misguided and potentially dangerous. The new assessments, they charged, were too new and untried—and too reliant on teachers' judgments rather than on objective means—to be used for such purposes as determining whether students would graduate from high school. And, the critics said, the standards themselves were wrongheaded: what was needed was not problem-solving abilities but knowledge of a core body of information. Rather than experiment with new systems, the critics argued, the schools should strengthen what they had for years done well—go "back to basics," as their campaign slogan put it. And to the many residents who considered the Littleton schools exemplary, this idea rang true.

The Backlash Against Standards/Assessment Reform

The clash between the two competing visions of education that made the 1993 Littleton school board race so heated has recurred in a number of cities and states around the country. Change is usually unsettling, particularly in districts whose supporters consider themselves successful already. But the new standards and assessment systems that school districts and states have implemented have ignited particularly vociferous challenges.

There are several reasons for this. First, the reforms are deliberately designed to make explicit what in most schools is unknown: the expectations for student learning. Schools seldom consider what they expect students to know and be able to do when they emerge, let alone publicize those expectations. The only way anyone outside the system can find out what is being taught is to read textbooks, and except for a handful of activists who challenge material in the books, few read them closely. And textbooks indicate only what goes into the system—what teachers teach. They do not show what students learn. Tests, the method schools use to determine what students have learned, are deliberately kept secret, in order to prevent cheating.

The new systems, by contrast, are intended to be open at nearly every stage. By setting standards in a public way, schools invite participants to buy into the reforms and adopt them as their own. And, many argue, the type of secrecy that surrounds traditional testing makes it impossible for students to reach the standards; only by knowing up front the type of performance schools expect can students hope to attain it. But as a result of their openness, the explicit standards invite challenge and argument.

A second reason for the intense debate over standards and new assessments is the kind of student performance the new systems hope to engender. Driven by research on how children learn and by the demands from business and elsewhere for higher levels of abilities among young people, the designers of the new systems are calling for teaching and learning that are substantially different from the kind of instruction most adults know. In place of the traditional model—in which the teacher imparts knowledge to students, who generally sit in rows and work alone at their desks—the reformers envision classrooms in which students work in groups and take responsibility for their own learning, with the teacher serving more as a coach to help them along. The teacher's role shifts from that of a "sage on the stage" to a "guide on the side."

This vision, however, appears threatening to people who consider the purpose of education to master a body of knowledge. This perceived threat is particularly acute among religious conservatives who look upon the Bible as the revealed truth, which is why some Christian activists have fought the new systems and why People for the American Way attempted to find out if there was a religious motive behind the candidates in Littleton.

Moreover, the critics are leery of the assessments schools are using to measure higher-level knowledge and skills. Instead of asking students questions and telling them to choose the correct answer, schools and states are asking students to generate their own problems and their own responses—by writing essays, analyzing works of literature or historical events, or writing science laboratory reports. Teachers then evaluate student performances against standards that teachers have agreed upon. To skeptics accustomed to machine-scored multiple-choice tests, these assessments may appear less rigorous academically. At the same time, some object that the assessments intrude upon families by asking students to write about their personal lives.

Despite these objections, though, the number of places moving toward creating new standards and assessment systems is growing.

And it will only continue to grow, particularly in the wake of the Clinton Administration's Goals 2000: Educate America Act, which offers financial incentives for states to develop standards and new assessments. But as the architects of these systems put them into place, they must overcome substantial hurdles. As the Littleton example shows, they face political opposition from those who remain wary of the new systems and thus must make the case in the political arena that the systems are necessary to produce high levels of learning among all students. And the advocates of the new methods must also demonstrate that the new instruments are technically sound and indeed provide valid, reliable, and fair measures of what students know and are able to do. As the saying goes, schools are now attempting to build airplanes and fly them at the same time.

We will examine several examples of systems that are already in place and consider in detail the obstacles that they and the other architects face. But first let us look more closely at the Littleton system and what it was attempting to do.

"Peak Performance" at Littleton's Mark Twain

The modular walls of Mark Twain Elementary School in Littleton, Colorado, are papered with student-made posters. The posters cover a broad range of topics—how chimpanzees and people are alike, how wooden baseball bats are made, how parrots learn to talk—and they include a variety of materials, from photographs to drawings to text, that attempt to provide answers.

To prepare the posters, pupils spend a week during class time researching their topic, which they choose in consultation with their teachers. They also prepare a written presentation on the topic, as well as an oral version that they present to a team consisting of their teacher, the school principal, and a representative of the community. Each part of the package is scored according to standards developed by the teachers.

This is the new way of knowing what young people know, Mark Twain–style. Developed locally, the program shares many of the characteristics of the new methods that are beginning to crop up around the country. It allows students to address real-world questions, not abstract exercises. It permits them to demonstrate complex thinking, not isolated skills. And it taps a variety of abilities, not just a narrow range of skills that are easy to measure by traditional means.

The assessment, which has been in place at Twain since 1989, has already transformed teaching in the school. In fact, teachers are so focused on getting students to pose their own questions and solve problems that they are not sure how the students will do on tests that demand factual recall. "I don't teach that way," says Jan May, a first-grade teacher. "My kids don't fill in answers. They don't choose from among four answers."[2] But she and others do not hesitate to add that they would not have it any other way.

Located in a relatively affluent suburb south of Denver, Twain has 450 pupils in kindergarten through grade five. It began its quest for a new method of defining and measuring student performance in 1987, after the school board adopted a policy requiring each Littleton school to develop a strategic plan for improvement. In formulating its plan, Twain first chose a vision for the school that stated that the students, the staff, and the school as a whole should strive for "peak performance." The school defined peak performance as "the fusion of thought and action to achieve significant goals that were presumed to be beyond the reach of a person."

"Almost everyone agrees that human beings possess far more potential and talents than are ever used," a statement prepared by the school states. "Peak performance is putting these dormant abilities into action. It involves both the mind and the heart of a person, and requires a work ethic intent upon constant growth and self-improvement."[3]

Twain thus began by defining the end "product" of schooling: what kind of person should emerge from the school. While such a step appears simple, it is unfortunately rare in schools. And it is getting harder and harder to accomplish as society continues to load problems onto schools. Whenever a social problem emerges—whether it is traffic safety, low productivity in the workplace, or the AIDS epidemic—schools become the front line of defense. They become driver-education centers, worker-training centers, condom-distribution centers, and many other things, including academic institutions. And their mission gets murkier and murkier.

In carrying out its vision, the Twain staff agreed to make substantial changes in the school's organization and programs. They gave teachers and parents a stronger role in setting policies. They reorganized the teaching staff into "clusters" that work together and stay with students for two or three years. They established before- and after-school programs and collaborations with the public library. They significantly stepped up the use of computers and other technologies.

A key element of the new structure, though, was a new assessment system. It was aimed explicitly at focusing instruction and defining standards for student performance. Twain's assessments, according to the school's statement, would "call for students to provide real-life demonstrations of mastery and go well beyond the information provided by multiple-choice achievement tests."[4]

The school did not, however, abandon conventional tests. Instead, it combined information from those tests, the new assessments, and other sources to develop a more well rounded portrait of the pupils' achievement. As Kenneth Turner, the school's current principal, explains, "No single indicator provides the entire picture of a child's performance. They're like bathing suits: They're revealing in what they show, but what's crucial is what they hide."[5]

In creating the new system, the teachers and administrators developed assessments in reading, writing, and thinking skills. They plan to add others in science, mathematics, and the arts as well. All of the new assessments reflect the ideas emerging from research on how to measure and evaluate student performance. They ask students to actively demonstrate what they know and can do. They are connected directly to classroom instruction and to the world outside of the classroom. And they are judged according to agreed-upon standards for what students should know and be able to do.

In one third-grade writing assessment, for example, students are asked to read a story, *The Sign of the Beaver*, by Elizabeth George Speare, and then, over several class sessions, to discuss with their teacher and classmates the ideas in the story. Following the discussion sessions, the students are asked to write an essay about a particular passage in the story. In their essay, which students are given an afternoon to complete, the students are expected to state their opinions and to support them with details, examples, and incidents from the story as well as with their own ideas and beliefs. The essays are scored on a 0-to-4 scale, with 4 the top score, according to three dimensions: content and style, the use of language conventions, and the use of the writing process (that is, the extent to which they plan and revise their work). For example, raters—teachers, school administrators, and professional writers—assess the degree to which students clearly state their opinions, provide support for their opinions, use expressive language, write fluently and articulately, and state their conclusion thoughtfully. They also judge whether students use complete sentences and use words, grammar, spelling, and punctuation correctly.

Similarly, thinking-skills assessments also ask students to complete a task. For example, students are given two identical sets of colored chips. One set is placed on a table before them; the other is in a bag. In one-on-one discussions with their teachers, the students are asked to select chips from the bag after predicting the color of each chip they will select and explaining their predictions. Their responses are then rated on a four-point scale. Those rated as demonstrating "formal" thinking skills make predictions based on deductive reasoning they can explain, use mathematical equations to calculate probability, and refine their answers as they go along; those demonstrating "concrete" skills use simple logic; and those demonstrating "preoperational" skills display little or no consideration of relationships and variables. The final rating is for students who make no response.

The heart of the new assessment system, however, is the research assessment—the one that produces the posters that line the walls. While students in all grades take the subject-matter assessments, the research assessment was designed originally as a "culminating" activity for fifth-graders. Teachers expect everything students have learned through the fifth grade—from their content knowledge to their abilities to research, write, and speak—to go into the project. It has since been expanded to include students in the earlier grades as well.

A key aspect of the assessment is allowing the students to choose their own topics. According to the teachers, students who select their research topics are more motivated to do a good job and less likely to resist or to act out than those who have topics handed to them.

Some research suggests that the teachers may be right: that students who are motivated to do well on tests perform better than those who are not. In a study of eighth-graders taking part in the National Assessment of Educational Progress, researchers from the National Center for Research on Evaluation, Standards, and Student Testing offered one group of students a financial incentive to do well on the tests—$1 for each correct answer—while another group received an instruction that read, "By doing the best you can, you will be making an important contribution." The students offered the cash award outperformed the other group, particularly on easier test questions, and reported putting more effort into their task. However, the study found that the financial incentive made no difference in twelfth-graders' performance.[6]

Students at Twain seem to agree that choosing their topics motivates them to work harder. Some have chosen topics related to their parents' occupations, such as one boy who examined the "brains" behind a microcomputer; another child, with an interest in art, opted to study what inspired great artists; still another selected a topic related to Albert Einstein, a personal hero. But this feature does not mean that anything goes. Teachers consult with students on their selection and often guide them toward topics that will bring out their investigative and problem-solving abilities. One student, for example, had proposed researching the question, "What are the different types of cats?" But her teacher, Margie Zyzda, let her know that such a question would produce a list, not an investigation. The teacher suggested that the student instead examine how the various cats are different or compare lions and domestic cats.[7]

Once students select their topics, they spend every afternoon for a week gathering information. They then write their reports on a computer, develop a visual representation of their findings (usually a poster), and prepare a five-minute oral presentation. In this way, the research assessment blurs the line between assessment and instruction. "Taking" the assessment becomes doing interesting and instructive classroom work; preparing students for the assessment becomes good teaching. Thus assessments can improve instruction as teachers do what they would naturally do: prepare students to do well on the assessment.

Judges evaluate the written papers on the same 0-to-4 scale used for the writing assessment. They also rate the oral presentations on a 0-to-4 scale on the following dimensions:

1. Student clearly describes the question and gives reasons for its importance.	Student states question, but does not describe it or give reasons for its importance.	Student does not state question.
2. Evidence of preparation and organization strong.	Some evidence of preparation and organization present.	No evidence of preparation or organization.

3. Delivery engaging.	Delivery somewhat engaging.	Delivery flat.
4. Sentence structure is correct.	Sentence structure is somewhat correct.	Sentence structure has many errors.
5. Visual aid used to enhance presentation.	Visual aid referred to separately.	Visual aid is not mentioned.
6. Questions from audience answered clearly and with specific information.	Questions from audience somewhat answered.	Questions from audience not answered.

Using a similar scoring guide, the raters also judge the visual presentation on the degree to which it is eye-appealing, presents important information about the question, can stand alone and be a useful source of information, uses artistic strategies effectively, and is well organized.

With the help of a foundation grant, the teachers developed the scoring guides, known as rubrics, over a year-and-a-half period of intense discussion. They divided themselves into groups to come up with guides for each assessment, making sure that each group included one member of a team-teaching pair to ensure that the information spread throughout the faculty. Once they wrote the rubrics and felt that they understood what the standards were, they went back to the drawing board and rewrote them so that students, too, would be able to understand them. They knew that students would have to be aware of the standards so that they could strive to attain them as they did their work.

According to the teachers, at least, the assessment has succeeded in providing better information than conventional tests about student abilities. The assessment has greater validity, says Barbaralynn Bitzer. "We see how much [students] do know, instead of [how much they are] guessing."[8]

Armed with such information, teachers can share their understanding about students' abilities and do a better job of preparing their lessons. Unlike teachers at most schools, who are isolated from one another and seldom meet with their colleagues, teachers at Twain meet regularly to talk about the students in their "clusters." The assessment information gives them a basis upon which to discuss students.

Beyond providing better information, the new assessments have also transformed teaching at Mark Twain Elementary School. No longer are teachers the sole source of knowledge; instead, students take responsibility for their own learning. Teachers seldom rely on textbooks anymore; in fact, the school has stopped ordering workbooks for mathematics classes. The teachers are more like coaches, guiding their students as they develop their skills and seek out their knowledge. "I'm not the one telling them what to do," says Barbaralynn Bitzer. "I almost take a back seat and let them go."[9]

Giving students responsibility also means making them aware of the standards for performance, something that is new for Twain and most schools. As Monte Moses, the former principal, notes, "Before, we simply gave assignments. Students received grades, but we didn't specify *why* they were graded in any specific way. Now, the standard is rigorously explained. We send them through trial runs to get them ready, and after they do it once we do it again. . . . The idea is for [students] to get better at it, know what the standards are, and chart their improvement."[10]

The idea of an open standard is one of the key differences between the old and new methods of assessment. Before, when students were judged solely on whether they answered questions correctly or not, the standards—the right answers—had to remain secret to prevent cheating. Even the questions had to remain secure, to ensure that no student had an unfair advantage.

Judging students according to standards of performance, on the other hand, demands openness, so that the public feels confident in a school's standards and students have a fair opportunity of meeting them. This idea is not new. In other countries, examination questions that represent the standard for graduation from secondary school are printed in newspapers and become a major topic of discussion. But in the United States, notes Grant Wiggins, a leader in the movement toward alternative assessments, standardized testing grew because schools seldom grappled with the issue of setting standards. He maintains that

> reform of testing depends . . . on teachers' recognizing that standardized testing evolved and proliferated because the school transcript became untrustworthy. An "A" in "English" means only that some adult thought the student's work was excellent. Compared to what or whom? As determined by what criteria? In reference to what specific subject matter? . . .
>
> To regain control over both testing and instruction, schools need to rethink their diploma requirements and grades. They need a clear set of appropriate and objective criteria, enabling both students *and outsiders* to know what counts, what is essential—what a school's standards really are. Until we specify what students must demonstrate to earn a diploma, they will continue to pass by meeting the de facto "standard" of being dutiful and persistent—irrespective of the quality of their work.[11]

The idea of giving children responsibility for their learning may be daunting for those teachers who are accustomed to staying in control of their classrooms, as well as for students used to following rules. But it is consistent with the notion from cognitive science that learners construct their own knowledge based on what they already know. Giving students responsibility also helps develop skills they will need throughout their lives. "We want to put ourselves out of business," says Kenneth Turner, with only slight exaggeration. "We want self-propelled learners."[12]

Although the system is relatively new, there is some anecdotal evidence that it has begun to attain its ultimate goal: to raise the level of student achievement. According to Jan May, students who went through the research assessment in fourth grade are posing much more sophisticated questions for the fifth-grade assessment. In addition, she says, the students appear much more intellectually engaged. "Children talk differently to you now about their books because they're not just reciting and calling back simple facts to you. Now they're telling us more about what they're reading and why they're reading it. They're describing relationships between characters more fully."[13]

Moreover, despite the teachers' fears that the pupils' performance on standardized tests might suffer under the new system, students at Twain continue to attain high scores on those tests.

Parents, too, say they believe the new system has been beneficial. In a community-wide survey in 1993, which a remarkable 80 percent of parents completed, about 80 percent of the respondents said they believed that the performance assessments would help prepare their children for the future.

Despite such positive signs, however, Mark Twain Elementary School's new assessment system has not been a complete success. The school had to go back to the drawing board to create a science-literacy assessment after the one that teachers had originally designed proved too cumbersome. The original plan involved a three- to four-week investigation of a "meaningful question about a topic of scientific interest"—a block of time that turned out to be too long in practice.

The new system has also encountered resistance from some parents who are unsure about the shift to a new way of knowing what students know. Although the school took pains to inform parents about what they were doing and why, and most parents appeared to support the shift, a few raised objections. The critics particularly objected to a new report card the school developed to show a range of students' abilities in different subjects rather than simple letter grades. The report card includes marks in ninety-five categories—for example, seven separate areas under "mathematical concepts and processes": the extent to which the student knows basic computation facts in each of the four arithmetic operations, shows an understanding of place value, knows when and how to use appropriate mathematical operations and the solution of word problems, uses a variety of strategies to solve math problems, uses a calculator appropriately in the solution of math problems, checks own work for accuracy and neatness, and applies mathematical concepts to daily living.

In an editorial, however, the *Rocky Mountain News* said the report card smacks of "professional shop talk." "It is apparently the wave of the future," the newspaper stated, "or, in the current lexicon, an example of the 'new age' of report cards, heavy on measurements of 'self-esteem' and 'wellness' and rather short on whether Johnny knows the location of the Ukraine."[14]

But the criticism appeared to die down as parents got used to the new report card and discovered that it does indeed provide more information about their children's performance. A local television station broadcast a report at the end of the year that highlighted parents' satisfaction with the report card; and a survey by the school found that three-fourths of the parents polled felt the report card represents an improvement over the old system.

One question remaining for the school is whether the assessments, which have proved valuable instructional tools, can also serve as valid and reliable measures of student performance. If not, the results cannot be credible indicators of what children know and are able to do. The challenge of building assessments that are technically sound is a major hurdle. And as the experience in nearby high schools shows—an experience we turn to now—it could bring down the entire system.

A New Standard for Graduation at
Littleton High School

Like students at many large high schools, ninth-graders entering Littleton High School's class of 1995 received a thick course catalogue outlining the choices they would have over the next four years. But a closer look would have revealed a significant difference from most such volumes. In addition to the course titles and descriptions, the Littleton High School catalogue also indicated how each course would prepare students in the skills and knowledge they would be expected to demonstrate. Littleton High School, like its cross-town counterpart Mark Twain, created a new way of measuring student performance: rather than giving students a traditional test that says little about what they know and can do, the school defined the skills and knowledge all students would be expected to have and created new assessments to allow them to demonstrate that they had attained such abilities.

As originally designed, the reforms at Littleton High School—and at nearby Heritage High School—represented a radical departure from traditional school practice. For nearly a century, high schools have defined student progress by time, in units known as "Carnegie units." A student takes four years of English, three each of science, social studies, and math, and a few electives, and earns a diploma. In the past decade, when states wanted to toughen standards, they added a few more required courses. But those mandates affected only the "inputs" of the system. They said nothing about the "outcomes": what students should know and be able to do when they leave. A student may take a test that says little about what she knows and is able to do. The diploma she will be given indicates nothing about her skills and knowledge, and she has little incentive, unless she is bound for a selective college, to do any more than passing work in her classes. As a brochure prepared by Littleton High School puts it: "If Johnny is able to sit through four years of English and a few other basic subjects, and fake his way through a few simple tests, he's got himself a diploma and a tassel for his rearview mirror. All he needs to do is show up and make a minimal effort, and chances are, he'll pass. Which is all the system encourages him to do. Pass. But not excel."[15]

But that is not good enough, the educators agreed, even in a district such as Littleton, where more than 80 percent of graduates go on to higher education. They felt that young people, to be prepared for the future, needed to know how to solve problems, reason, and communicate—precisely the "thinking curriculum" that the cognitive scientist Lauren B. Resnick says should be available to everyone (a topic discussed in greater detail in Chapter Three). And, recognizing the influence of testing on school practice, the Littleton schools agreed to set goals for student performance and design assessments aligned with the goals.

In the case of Littleton High School, a 1,400-student school for grades nine through twelve, teachers and administrators began by assessing what was *right* with the school. They noted that they had, among other assets, a talented staff, a community that valued high-quality education, and a diverse student body that had done well on traditional measures of achievement. But they also pointed out that the current system had become a barrier to learning. The community would no longer support an outmoded system, the Littleton educators concluded. Therefore, they developed a vision statement, just as their counterparts at Mark Twain had. The statement read,

America needs young people who know how to learn, as well as how to read, write, speak, and compute. America needs young people with strong interpersonal skills, the ability to contribute to economic productivity and social progress and justice. America needs young people who can acquire, analyze, and apply information, so as to think creatively and solve problems.

As workers, parents, citizens, and individuals, members of the next generation should know how to question, invent, anticipate, and dream.

We of the Littleton High School community should work every day to help young people do these things, so that they can move, at last, beyond us, each prepared to make a living, make a life, and make a difference.

Toward those ends, the school created what it called Direction 2000, a performance-based system of education. At the heart of the system was the shift from "seat time" to outcomes. Specifically, teachers, teams of teachers, administrators, and parents developed nineteen skills that students were required to master in order to graduate. They included requirements that students write articulately and effectively, that they effectively apply mathematical principles and operations to solve a range of problems, and that they use research and the problem-solving process to make distinctions and arrive at decisions. The new rules also required students to understand the importance of ethical conduct and to interact well and work cooperatively with others.

For each graduation requirement, teachers and administrators developed a set of "demonstrations" that would enable students to show that they had attained the outcomes. Under the plan, students were required, prior to graduation, to attain proficiency in all nineteen areas and excellence in any two, as shown in the demonstrations. The requirement for excellence was aimed at allowing students to show distinction in the areas in which they are most talented while also sending a message to all students to strive for excellence. One student might show particular interest and abilities in mathematics or science, another in performing arts, and another in athletics, says Littleton's principal, Tim Westerberg. "We want to establish the habit of mind that, when you leave here, you are good at something. It's not OK just to be proficient at everything."[16]

The demonstrations were performance-based assessments that asked students to write, conduct experiments, solve problems, or in some other way use their knowledge, not just find the correct answer. As an example, the following is a demonstration task developed to measure the requirement that students speak and write effectively:

> Student writes a letter to a public policy maker regarding the official's position on a current political issue, presenting the student's opinion and persuading the public policy maker to vote accordingly. The public policy maker is opposed to the student's position. Students will be provided documentation of public policy maker's position and background information. Student will be given a choice of several situations.

According to the school's standards, in a "proficient" demonstration,

- The letter is persuasive; the writer clearly states an opinion, uses facts to support the opinion, and explains why the facts support the opinion.
- Acceptable letter format is used.
- The argument is "one-sided"—the writer does not successfully use facts to refute the public policy maker's.
- Basic organization of the letter is presentation of a problem and discussion of a solution.
- Wording and attitude are appropriately formal for writing a public policy maker.
- Few grammatical, punctuation, or spelling errors; these errors do not detract from the purpose or organization of the letter.
- Vocabulary is sufficient and the sentence structure is complex, but not varied.

By contrast, in an "excellent" response,

- Letter is persuasive; writer clearly states an opinion, uses facts to support the opinion, and explains why the facts support the opinion.

- In addition, also presents a "two-sided" argument—explaining why the facts support the writer's opinion and refute the public policy maker's.

- Writer often uses psychological motivator ("Why you're off-the-wall if you don't support my position").

- Basic organization is presentation of a problem, discussion of a solution, and recommendation for an action.

- Wording and attitude are appropriately formal for writing a public policy maker.

- Letter is essentially free of grammatical, punctuation, and spelling errors.

- Vocabulary is interesting, sentence structure is varied.

Those responses that were deficient in some way—lacking persuasiveness or showing poor organization, inappropriate wording, frequent errors, weak vocabulary—would be considered "unacceptable."[17]

At Heritage High School, meanwhile, about twenty teams consisting of some 200 teachers and parents developed thirteen graduation requirements and fifty tasks to gauge whether students could demonstrate that they had met the requirements. Unlike Littleton's plan, the Heritage program required students to demonstrate only proficiency on every task, not excellence. A draft of a science task, for example, required students to conduct an experiment in class and to write a laboratory report on the results. To meet the standard for proficiency, students were required, in conducting the experiment, to follow safety rules and teacher-approved procedures, show proper use of materials and equipment, work independently, collect original data, and make minor adjustments if necessary. In writing the lab report, students had to identify the purpose, state the hypothesis, outline the procedure, identify the control and the variables, organize the data in chart, graph, or tabular form, state the results, and draw a conclusion, all the while addressing the biological, chemical, or physical aspects of the experiment.

Like Mark Twain's assessments, these high school demonstrations represented a substantial shift in the way the schools gauged student performance. The assessments involved real-world problems, and they asked students to engage in complex thinking and to use a broad range of abilities. And in preparing students to do well on the tasks, teachers engaged in the type of instruction that enhances learning.

But the new systems were intended to do more than that. For Littleton, where the system was put in place in 1991, effective for the class of 1995, the reform became a way of restructuring the entire school to focus on improving student performance. Before, teachers concede, students understood that their learning depended on which teacher they were assigned. Some teachers challenged their students, but others allowed them to get by without doing much work. Teachers might introduce a new technique if they happened to attend a seminar on a particular topic, such as teaching writing, but otherwise they generally taught the way they had always taught.

By contrast, as the new system was put in place, teachers worked together to define the standards for student performance— a process that made teachers feel engaged professionally. "This place is so much more stimulating than ever before," says Daniel Brickley, a social studies teacher. "It was a deadly place for decades."[18] The discussions also produced substantial changes in school organization and teaching practices. The school instituted an "advisement" program, under which entering freshmen were assigned a faculty adviser, who counseled them throughout their four-year career on their coursework to help prepare them to meet the graduation requirements. The school also redesigned its in-service training to support the standards. Teachers would take a seminar when they felt they needed it, not just when an expert happened to be in town.

Teachers also began to discuss ways of forging links across disciplines, a major step for high schools, which are usually organized according to subject area. As the saying goes, elementary teachers teach children, but high school teachers teach math, science, or English. But at Littleton, the graduation requirements encouraged teachers to cross the great divides and consider teaching in a more interdisciplinary way. By writing the demonstrations in such a way that students could fulfill an English requirement in a history class, for example, teachers encouraged history and English instruction to merge, as well as coursework in many other areas. The course catalogue was intended to guide students through the process, so that they could see how their course of study could lead to the desired outcomes.

Most in the Littleton High School community hailed the changes, and indeed the program attracted teachers and parents from around the state. But the reforms proved a hard pill to swallow for some teachers and students. One teacher took her objections to the local newspaper. In a letter to the *Littleton Independent*, Linda Young, an English teacher, wrote of her "grave doubts" about the plan. She contended that the outcomes would be "all but impossible to evaluate," that the advisement program was a "waste of potentially useful academic time," and that the instructional changes were ill-advised. "'Lecture' is a dirty word as we focus ever more on 'cooperative learning,' a slow process of teaching where the 'blind lead the blind' as standardized test scores fall."[19]

Students accustomed to the traditional methods of teaching and school organization, in which teachers impart facts to them and tell them what to do at every step, also found the changes a rude awakening. Daniel Brickley, the social studies teacher, says many of his students, including honors students, were at first "unable to cope" with a task that required them to use the past to explain the present and anticipate the future, one of the nineteen requirements. "Eleventh-graders have never been asked to use anything they've learned," he says. "Many of them were absolutely lost."[20]

To earn and keep students' and parents' support for the changes, the school had to ensure that the new system was a valid and reliable way of knowing what young people know. School officials took steps in that direction. For one thing, they solicited reactions from college admissions officials, who indicated that the demonstrations would provide a better way than the existing system of knowing what applicants know and are able to do.

But those actions failed to assuage the concerns of another group of parents, who remained unconvinced that the new assessments could validly and reliably judge student performance. Led by William Cisney, a local fabric-store retailer whose son attended Heritage High School, the parents directed an attack on the new system. First, Cisney and Carol Brzeczek, another parent of a Heritage student, attended the meetings of Heritage's central committee, which directed that school's reforms, and prepared a set of "alternative" minutes that criticized many of the proceedings. Then, contending that parents and community representatives were insufficiently involved in the decisions, Cisney and Brzeczek filed a lawsuit charging the school with violating the state's "sunshine law," which requires public participation in governmental decisions.

But in their most decisive—and successful—step, the two parents, along with John Fanchi, the parent of a middle school student, teamed up to run for the three contested seats on the school board. If victorious, they would take control of the five-member board and suspend the new graduation requirements in the high schools.

The trio maintained that the pioneering effort in the district to create standards and new assessments would impose on students an untried experiment with potentially disastrous consequences. In its place, the group argued for a return to "traditional education," or an emphasis on basic skills and knowledge. "Being first," the candidates argued in a joint position paper, "means that our children will be subjected to new programs with no track record and no proven merit. Our schools will be making the mistakes for the rest of the country."[21]

Immediately following victory, the back-to-basics contingent set out to change the schools' policies. However, despite fears of educators, they did not throw out everything the schools had done.

Although they eliminated the use of new assessments as graduation requirements in Littleton and Heritage High Schools and prohibited assessments in such areas as personal attitudes and values, the board members permitted the schools to continue to use new assessments within classrooms and allowed Mark Twain and the other elementary schools to use their new assessments. Thus, while the election slowed the movement toward a new method of assessing what young people know and can do, it did not derail it entirely. And, as schools in other school districts have shown, the movement continues.

Growth and Reflection at San Diego's O'Farrell Community School

Sitting in small groups, the seventh- and eighth-graders in Lenora Smith's language arts class at O'Farrell Community School in San Diego are discussing some of their recent work.

The students have written papers on the "O'Farrell Way," a set of principles that guide the school, and have created comic strips that attempt to explain the school to outsiders. At most schools, the students' work would end once they turned in their papers to their teachers. But not at O'Farrell. There students also engage in "personal reflection"—considering what they have learned from their work and whether they have met their expectations. They also seek feedback from peers and adults and make revisions based on the comments they receive. They then place the work in a portfolio, which they will show to a panel of teachers and community members as evidence that they have met the school's standards for graduation from eighth grade.

Along with projects (such as the Mark Twain research projects) and performance tasks (such as the demonstrations at Littleton High School), portfolios represent the third category of new types of student assessment. In some ways, they hold the most promise of all. In addition to providing the opportunity for authentic work on complex, real-life problems, portfolios also allow students to show

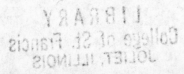

their development over time. And they offer the chance for self-evaluation.

As Dennie Palmer Wolf (a Harvard University researcher who is the head of a national project that includes O'Farrell) notes, the kind of reflection the students there engage in is rare in schools but common in the world in which adults live. As she points out, figures as diverse as the baseball pitcher Orel Hershiser, the sculptor Ree Morton, and the jazz saxophonist Sonny Rollins all practice some form of "reflective self-evaluation."

"Never do we stop to ask how we could make our evaluative gate-keeping model the kind of self-observation and informed critique that separates ball-tossers from fine pitchers, doodlers from artists, or instrumentalists from musicians. Yet virtually every student walks out of school into years of long-term projects: raising children, building a house, running a farm, writing a novel, or becoming a better lab technician. All of these projects require moment-to-moment monitoring, Monday-morning quarterbacking, and countless judgments of errors and worth. Unfortunately, very little in the way we now structure assessment in schools names or encourages those lifelong skills."[22]

Of course, portfolio assessment is only one aspect of the reform effort that has made O'Farrell one of the most popular destinations for educators nationwide. In fact, the school has received so many visitors that it has incorporated the visits into the curriculum: in order to graduate, all students must conduct at least one tour of the school and demonstrate an understanding of its philosophy and goals.

But the portfolios are indeed central to its mission. As the school's full title indicates, O'Farrell is more than a school; it is a "center for advanced academic studies." It demands high levels of academic performance by every student, and such demands require a new way of knowing what students know.

Unlike the Littleton schools, which reformed themselves, O'Farrell began from scratch as a restructured school. Created to occupy a school building that had recently been vacated, O'Farrell

was the product of a team of educators and community leaders—
including the "chief educational officer" (or principal), Robert
Stein—who called themselves the "dream team." Working for more
than a year before the school opened its doors in 1990, the team
designed a school that was far removed from conventional practice.
They elected to do away with the positions of assistant principal
and counselor and to use the funds instead to hire additional teachers and reduce class sizes. They created an on-site family support
services wing to provide health and social services to students who
did not receive those services elsewhere. They divided the school
into nine "families," each composed of about 150 students and half
a dozen teachers. They established an advisement system that gave
each student a "home base."

But the primary mission of the school was to provide each student with the opportunity to learn at high levels, and the founders
set for themselves an ambitious goal: every student would graduate
from eighth grade ready to do advanced coursework in high school.
This would be a daunting task at any school, but at O'Farrell it
proved especially challenging, because O'Farrell is the type of school
where students are not expected to succeed academically. Located
in a section of San Diego where gangs and drugs are prevalent,
O'Farrell draws from a lower-income and minority population that
in most places lags behind more affluent peers in school. More than
half the students are eligible for federal Chapter I remedial aid, and
about a fourth of the area's eighth-grade students drop out before
graduating from high school. About a third of the 1,300 students at
O'Farrell are African American, a third are Filipino, a fifth are His-
panic, and fewer than a tenth are white.

To help the students achieve their academic aims, the teachers
and the CEO redesigned teaching and learning, based on a new way
of knowing what young people know. At the heart of the new system was the "O'Farrell Standard," a set of tasks that all students
must complete in order to graduate. According to this standard, all
students must do the following: complete the equivalent of twelve

hours of community service each year; present an exhibition to a panel of teachers, parents, peers, and community members that demonstrates evidence of their academic, social, and personal growth; complete a research project; conduct a school tour; demonstrate academic competence in reading, written self-expression, mathematical reasoning, and research; and demonstrate practice of the O'Farrell Way.

To gather evidence that they have met this challenge, students compile a portfolio of their work over the course of their O'Farrell career. Among other elements, the portfolios consist of a dozen items per semester, including at least one from every subject area, and the personal reflections and peer and adult reviews Lenora Smith's seventh- and eighth-graders were completing.

As at Mark Twain and at Littleton High School, where the new assessments reshaped instruction, the portfolios at O'Farrell turned out to be much more than new tests. They helped forge what Dennie Palmer Wolf calls a "portfolio culture." In order to help students gather material to show that they have met the O'Farrell Standard, teachers know that they cannot simply assign students chapters in textbooks and lists of questions at the end. Instead, students complete tasks that provide them the opportunity to demonstrate their abilities.

In addition, the portfolios also encourage teachers to make clear their own expectations for students. Clyde Yoshida, a math teacher, explains that he realized his students were not performing as well as they might because they were unaware of the standards. "I would see student work from other classes and say, 'Why can't my students write like that?' It's because of what I was doing," Yoshida says. Now he writes on the blackboard what he expects of his students—including their ability to write and explain their mathematical reasoning.[23]

At the same time, students are motivated to do well because they know that what they are doing in class will help them meet the standards for graduation. In many schools, teachers introduce assignments by saying, "Learn this; you'll need it in later life," when in fact the connection to a student's future is tenuous at best. At O'Farrell, though, teachers are explicit about how an assignment addresses a challenge in the O'Farrell Standard. Teachers also indicate the relevance of their classroom work by linking it to a common theme. For example, the theme might be the study of various cultures. In a language arts class, the students would read literature from the different cultures; in social studies, they would study their history and geography; in science, they might conduct tasks in genetics to show how physical traits pass from generation to generation within a culture.

In its short history, the portfolio program at O'Farrell has already undergone some revision. Teachers found that many parents lacked the time or expertise to conduct substantive evaluations of their children's work, so they scrapped the idea of requiring parents to respond to every piece. In addition, the school also ended the practice of asking students to characterize their work as evidence of "thinking," "feeling," or "creating," since they found that most pieces represented all three.

But despite those snags, the O'Farrell "dream team" has seen evidence that suggests that the program is succeeding. In accordance with the school's stated goal, many students, though not all, have qualified to enter advanced classes in high school. And students themselves say they see improvements in their own work. "When I look back on my work [from the previous year], it surprises me," says an eighth-grader. "I can do better."[24]

Other, more subtle indicators also point to success. The attendance rate has crept up, suggesting that students may be more willing than before to come to school. And teachers are volunteering to teach there, a rare step in that part of town.

Those improvements are impressive, and they confirm teachers' beliefs that setting standards and creating new assessments tied to the standards can transform classroom instruction. The real question for the new methods, however, is whether they can also serve as measures of student performance that will satisfy parents and the general public. In Littleton, it is over this question that the new systems met a wall of opposition.

Assessment Advances in Pittsburgh

Some school districts are taking steps to use new forms of assessment as *informational* as well as *instructional* devices. In Pittsburgh, for example, city officials in 1992 reported to the public for the first time information about student writing performance based on portfolios of their work. Pittsburgh already had some experience with using portfolios as instructional tools, however. Beginning in 1987, school officials teamed up with researchers from Harvard University and the Educational Testing Service to create Arts PROPEL, a Rockefeller Foundation–funded project to develop a method of using portfolios as a way of assessing student performance in the arts and humanities.

Like the O'Farrell portfolio assessments, the Arts PROPEL system was aimed at showing student growth over time and encouraging students to reflect on their work. And, as the O'Farrell teachers found, project officials in Pittsburgh discovered that student work improved as students developed a keen awareness of the standards for quality. But using the portfolios as external measures of student performance introduced a new set of demands. School officials had to ensure that the portfolios were valid, reliable, and fair measures of performance. And they had to convince the public that the results represented what students knew and were able to do.

To those ends, the Pittsburgh officials developed a set of standards against which to evaluate the portfolios and trained a group of teachers in applying the standards. Those teachers spent a week during the summer scoring portfolios from across the city. But the district also took another step: they asked a team of observers, including teachers from surrounding districts, community leaders, state officials, and national experts, to examine the process and reassure the public that the system was valid. With the observers' seal of approval, the Pittsburgh officials released the results.

State Participation in Assessment Reform

While a handful of schools and school districts have moved forward in developing new methods of measuring student performance, as the examples of this chapter show, it is at the state level that the most significant activity in redefining student assessment is taking place. Because of the large scale involved in state testing programs, new methods of assessment created by a state will have a far larger impact on classrooms than new assessments created by a school or a school district. The political hurdle (of garnering support for a new statewide system) and the educational hurdle (of ensuring that teachers are prepared to teach in the way the assessment demands) are correspondingly substantial. Moreover, creating a large-scale assessment poses special problems, particularly if the results of the assessment are used to hold students or schools accountable. States must ensure that the assessments indeed measure what students know and are able to do and are valid, reliable, and fair ways of measuring performance.

States are working through these issues, but in the meantime, several pioneering states have begun to put new assessment systems in place. We will examine a few of these in detail. But first let us consider how schools and states got to this point by examining how the testing enterprise has grown and how the problems with traditional tests have led to a quest for alternatives.

Chapter Two

One Hundred Fifty Years of Testing

Along with a small band of allies, Horace Mann, the leading educator of the mid-nineteenth century, had a vision for reforming education. Possessing a strong belief in the value of education as a tool for social advancement, Mann proposed the idea of a "common school" that would enable everyone—particularly the immigrants who were beginning to swell enrollments in Mann's home state of Massachusetts and elsewhere—to live fulfilling lives.

Like reformers everywhere, though, Mann faced opposition. His opponents consisted of teachers and headmasters who favored a classical education for an elite student body rather than the more practically oriented mass education Mann called for.

As the secretary of the Massachusetts State Board of Education, however, Mann had several weapons at his disposal; and the instrument he chose to help make his case was one that education policy makers would turn to again and again over the next century and a half: he created a test. More specifically, Mann, along with his ally Samuel Gridley Howe, in 1845 asked the Boston School Committee to administer a written examination to the city's schoolchildren, in place of the oral examinations teachers customarily used. The novel instrument, Mann and Howe reasoned, would provide objective information on the quality of teaching and learning in the city's schools.

In the short run, Mann and Howe's test helped their cause by exposing wide gaps in Boston students' knowledge. Armed with that information, city and state officials sharply criticized the school system and bolstered Mann's arguments for change. But in the long run, the greatest significance of the test was the success of the new instrument at measuring student performance. Unlike the oral examinations, which depended on a teacher's judgment, the written tests were "impartial" barometers of performance. The tests, Mann said, would "determine, beyond appeal or gainsaying, whether the pupils have been faithfully and competently taught."[1]

Confident about the power of the new instruments, Mann began to advocate the regular use of tests to monitor the quality of instruction and permit comparisons among teachers and schools. But as the use of tests as external information devices grew, so did the criticism of such uses. Teachers, in particular, increasingly questioned whether comparisons of school quality based on tests were fair.

If this account has a contemporary ring, it should. Many of the issues surrounding testing have changed little since Horace Mann's day. Tests have always loomed large in American education. To see how large, just walk into any classroom: when a teacher begins a new lesson, the first question students ask is, "Will this be on the test?" They will pay attention, or not, depending on the answer.

Savvy students know that what is on the test matters, because the test is how the rest of the world knows what they know and can do. While a student's grades may reflect a host of factors—from attendance to participation to willingness to clean the blackboard—the ultimate judgment about a student's level of achievement most often revolves around a test.

For teachers, tests have long served as a way to find out whether students have learned what they have been taught. Through the familiar end-of-chapter tests and weekly "pop quizzes," teachers can find out whether students can solve mathematics problems that employ the algebra concepts just covered or whether they can recall facts about the Gilded Age that were mentioned in the previous week's reading. Through midterm and final examinations, teachers can determine whether students have mastered the course material and are ready to move on to the next level.

As one recent survey confirmed, such classroom tests are a regular feature of instruction. Nearly nine out of ten middle school and secondary school math and science teachers polled said they use teacher-made tests at least once a month, while 70 percent of math teachers and 56 percent of science teachers said they use tests included in textbooks. And, as Richard J. Stiggins of the Northwest Regional Educational Laboratory estimates, between 20 and 30 percent of a teacher's professional time is directly involved with assessment-related activities. These include designing, developing, selecting, administering, scoring, recording, reporting, evaluating, and revising assignments, tests, quizzes, observations, and judgments about student performance.[2]

As the Horace Mann example shows, tests have played an important role outside of the classroom as well; and in many ways, it is these external tests—which often have high stakes attached to their use—that are the most significant ones students take. These tests communicate to school officials and to the public at large varied information about the state of students' and schools' performance. As any reader of the sports pages knows, Americans are fascinated by numerical rankings, and schools are not exempt from this obsession. Just as baseball fans pore over box scores to see how the home team's players are doing, public officials have sought to use tests to determine how students and schools are faring—and to use that information in setting education policy.

But like baseball statistics, test scores also provoke argument and debate. Many educators are leery of making judgments about young people's performance on the basis of tests, particularly the type that has dominated schooling for the past century and a half.

Since Horace Mann's day, we have relied on one method of finding out what young people know and are able to do: we take them out of the normal classroom setting and ask them questions that we have selected—questions representing a broad survey of the skills and knowledge in a subject area. We judge the answers—and only the answers (not the process by which they were derived)—

by determining whether they are right or wrong, removing as much as we can any judgment about the quality of the answers. We then compare how each student performed to how other students performed.

This method of finding out what students know has done more than provide information. Increasingly, it has shaped expectations for what students and teachers do every day in the classroom. Partly, this has happened by design: recognizing that everyone views tests as important, policy makers have increasingly relied on tests—commercially available tests such as the Iowa Test of Basic Skills and the Metropolitan Achievement Test, as well as tests developed by state departments of education—as a lever to improve performance. But as critics of the use of testing have been quick to point out, this power can exert a harmful influence on schools. In part, the movement to shift to a new method of testing is aimed at harnessing the power of tests toward positive ends.

An Emerging Technology

As schools began to grow into larger and larger enterprises in the late-nineteenth century, fueled in large part by massive waves of immigration, the interest among policy makers in tests as management tools grew rapidly. According to Lauren Resnick and Daniel Resnick, "Standardized tests in various school subjects were introduced into American schools in the period 1880–1920 when booming enrollments, large school-building programs, and the cult of efficiency in industry combined to encourage the schools to justify their performance in quantitative ways to local taxpayers. Short-answer and multiple-choice tests were viewed as cost-efficient and objective measures in which there might be some public confidence."[3]

Along with the growing interest in measuring student achievement grew the technology for doing so. One of the pioneers in demonstrating the power of standardized tests was Joseph Mayer Rice, a physician who had studied education in Germany. Interested in examining the effectiveness of teaching techniques, Rice developed tests in spelling, penmanship, English composition, and arithmetic, and he surveyed about 100,000 students in thirty-six cities. His findings, published in a national journal, shattered some myths; the spelling test, for example, showed that there was no relation between spelling achievement and the amount of time spent studying the subject.[4]

Led by such advances, achievement testing became codified into a science in the early years of the twentieth century. Its most influential voice was Edward L. Thorndike, a psychologist who attempted to apply to his nascent discipline the rigorous techniques of the "hard" sciences, such as physics and chemistry. As Thorndike was fond of saying, whatever exists, exists in quantity.

The use of testing in schools mushroomed following World War I, when the Army Alpha test—which was administered to more than 1.7 million soldiers—appeared to demonstrate the success of measuring intelligence. The Alpha test, a written test that asked recruits to solve analogies, complete sentences, and so forth, was intended to help the armed services place recruits into their proper ranks by demonstrating their mental qualifications. The Army also administered a separate test with figures, called the Beta test, for recruits deemed unable to read. But as with Horace Mann's Boston test, the significance of the Army tests was not so much in their immediate results—which appeared to show shockingly low levels of intelligence among recruits, particularly immigrants—as in the use of the instruments themselves. As Stephen Jay Gould, the biologist who wrote a stinging critique of the tests, wrote, the Army experiment demonstrated that "a technology had been developed for testing all pupils. Tests could now rank and stream everybody; the era of mass testing had begun."[5]

In the wake of that effort, schools clamored for intelligence tests to sort their students according to ability. But accompanying that wave was a rapid growth in the use of achievement tests to provide information on schools' effectiveness. The number of achievement tests available, which had risen steadily in the decade prior to World War I, increased tenfold in the 1920s. And a survey by the U.S. Bureau of Education showed that one key purpose of such tests was to gauge the quality of schools and teachers. Some 57 percent of the elementary schools in the 215 cities surveyed said the tests were used to compare their school with other school systems; 38 percent said they were used to judge the efficiency of teachers.[6]

Thus entrenched, testing became a regular feature of schooling. In 1929, the University of Iowa created the first statewide student tests, the Iowa Test of Basic Skills and the Iowa Test of Educational Development. Offered to schools on a voluntary basis—Iowa to this day is one of the few states that do not have a mandatory testing program—the Iowa tests provided student achievement information on a range of key subjects for grades three through high school. A decade later, the tests were offered to schools in other states as well, and they remain among the most often used commercially available achievement tests in the nation.

A pioneering effort in large-scale testing, the Iowa program was also largely responsible for making the practice cost-efficient and thus helped ensure testing's continued growth. In the 1950s, E. F. Lindquist, then the program's director, developed an electronic scoring machine that could read answer sheets, produce raw scores, and convert raw scores into standard scores, all in a fraction of the time—and cost—it took teachers and scientists to conduct those tasks by hand. Moreover, the machine also had the advantage of enhancing the seeming objectivity of test scores by removing teacher judgment from the picture altogether. At a time when Americans were growing increasingly fascinated by technological solutions to social problems, machine-scoring made testing almost irresistible.

The Second Wave

Fueled by such advances, the second wave of testing for external purposes—that is, outside the classroom—began in the 1960s and

has continued to crest to this day. Over the past three decades, public officials have increasingly relied on knowing what students know
to determine whether they are eligible for remedial or special education, for promotion to the next grade or graduation from high
school, or for special distinction, such as an honors diploma. Test
scores have also been used to decide if schools can earn cash
bonuses or freedom from state rules or if schools should be punished
by having their staff reassigned or by being taken over by the state.
The exploding interest in the use of tests, as we will see, has made
their method of measuring student performance critically important. But it has also generated a storm of criticism and demands for
a new method.

Two factors have helped drive the test engine of the last thirty
years. The first was a growing interest among education policy makers, beginning in the 1960s, in theories from business and public
administration that emphasized redesigning systems toward a goal.
These theories went by various names, including "planning, pro-
gramming, budgeting systems" and "management by objective."
Swept up in that wave, dozens of state legislatures passed legislation
that held schools accountable for raising student achievement—
the goal of the education system. At least seventy-three such laws
were enacted between 1963 and 1974.

One of the earliest and most comprehensive of these measures,
to take one example, was Florida's Education Accountability Act
of 1971. That statute directed the state's commissioner of education to establish education objectives for each subject area and
grade level and to develop a statewide testing system to determine
"the degree to which established educational objectives had been
achieved." Other state laws expressed similar objectives. In Colorado, the general assembly mandated a program to "measure objec-
tively the adequacy and efficiency of the educational programs
offered by the public schools." In Mississippi, lawmakers called for
the establishment of "an assessment of educational performance to
assist in the measurement of educational quality and to provide
information to school officials and citizens."[7]

Coinciding with the burgeoning interest in testing for account-ability in education was a gnawing anxiety among educators and citizens about the state of student achievement, which spurred another round of testing mandates. This anxiety reached a crescendo with the revelation that the average scores on the Scholastic Aptitude Test had declined by a total of 81 points between 1963 and 1977—from 478 points to 429 points on the ver-bal portion and from 502 points to 470 points on the math portion, both on a 200-to-800 scale.

This revelation shocked Americans and convinced them that their much-prized education system had slipped into steep decline. A commission was established by the College Board, the test's spon-sor, to investigate the cause of the decline. Commissioners con-cluded that "the public's interest is not in the psychometric technicalities of the S.A.T. score decline but in its implications regarding what is widely perceived as serious deterioration in learn-ing in America. More and more high school graduates show up in college classrooms, employers' personnel offices, or at other com-mon checkpoints with barely a speaking acquaintance with the English language and no writing facility at all. . . . Although the S.A.T. score figures are too small a window for surveying this broad condition, they provide special insight into it."[8]

The public reacted by calling for going "back to the basics," away from approaches that many considered less rigorous academ-ically—open classrooms and the "new math" among them. Accom-panying this movement was a demand for tests to ensure that students graduated from high school able to read, write, and com-pute. Responding to these pressures, thirty-six states adopted some form of "minimum competency" test to measure students' basic skills.

The demand for more and more testing did not abate. In fact, it increased in the early 1980s as part of the flood tide of education reform activity that followed the release of the landmark report *A Nation at Risk*. Commissioned by President Reagan's secretary of education, Terrel H. Bell, the report warned of a "rising tide of mediocrity" that threatened the nation's well-being. The report concluded ominously, "If an unfriendly foreign power had attempted to impose on America the mediocre educational performance that exists today, we might have viewed it as an act of war."

In one of its key recommendations, the report urged schools, colleges, and universities to adopt "more rigorous and measurable standards and higher expectations for student performance" and proposed tests as the appropriate measures. Standardized tests of achievement (not to be confused with aptitude tests) should be administered at major transition points from one level of schooling to another—particularly from high school to college or work—the report recommended. The purposes of these tests would be to (1) certify the student's credentials, (2) identify the need for remedial intervention, and (3) identify the opportunity for advanced or accelerated work. The report concluded that these tests should be administered as part of a nationwide (but not federal) system of state and local standardized tests.[9]

The report accelerated unprecedented school reform activity into high gear. Nearly every state adopted policies aimed at improving the schools within their borders—and many of these policies, heeding the report's recommendations, included the creation or expansion of statewide testing programs. A survey by the National Center for Research on Evaluation, Standards, and Student Testing at the University of California, Los Angeles, found that by 1984 thirty-nine states were operating at least one statewide testing program; by the end of the decade, this had risen to forty-seven states.[10]

This whirlwind of post–Nation at Risk reform activity at the state level did not supplant the testing that local school districts required; on the contrary, districts also upped their requirements in the 1980s. Governments layered policies on top of one another, with little coordination among them.

The federal government got into the act as well by expanding its testing program, the National Assessment of Educational

Progress. Created in 1969, NAEP, often called the "nation's report card," tested national samples of students in a range of subject areas. Beginning in the mid 1980s, however, state and national officials began to call for expanding the program to permit state-by-state, and perhaps even district-by-district, comparisons of student achievement. Such a move, according to a blue-ribbon panel appointed by William J. Bennett, who was the secretary of education, would improve NAEP's usefulness as a "rudder against the storm" of confusing information about the state of student achievement.

As the panel's report notes, the national assessment has been beneficial, but it suffers from a serious weakness: while providing excellent information on what our children know and can do, it provides it only for the nation as a whole and for very large regions of the country. "Whole-nation information is of course useful when we want to gauge the performance of our children against that of children in other countries, whether rivals or allies. But in the United States, education is a *state* responsibility, and it is against the performance of children closer to home that we want and need to compare the performance of our youngsters."[11]

Congress agreed to go along with the panel's recommendations for state-by-state comparisons, but on a trial basis only, and so far has rejected the idea of permitting district-level testing. In 1990, NAEP tested eighth-grade students in thirty-seven states in math; in 1992, it tested students in forty-four states in fourth-grade reading and fourth- and eighth-grade math.

As a result of all the legislation and rule-making, the number of tests students take in schools is staggering. The National Commission on Testing and Public Policy, a panel of educators and civil rights leaders created by the Ford Foundation, estimated in its 1989 report that the 41 million American students take 127 million tests a year—more than three tests a year for each student. In a survey of math and science teachers, researchers from Boston College found that 85 percent of elementary and middle school math teachers and 60 percent of elementary science teachers reported that one or more standardized tests were required of their students.

In a more cautious estimate, the General Accounting Office concluded that "systemwide" testing—tests given to all students, almost all students, or a representative sample of students at any one grade level in a school district—exerted only a modest burden on classroom time. The average student, the GAO estimated, spent only seven hours a year on testing, including preparation, test-taking, and all related activities.[12]

High Stakes

Whatever the actual number, though, the tests have become increasingly important, making the perennial student query—"Will this be on the test?"—ever more relevant. And in response to this trend, educators have become more vocal in questioning whether the tests reveal what young people know.

According to the Boston College survey, teachers' own tests play a vital role in shaping instruction. About two-thirds of the math teachers and three-fifths of the science teachers surveyed said their instruction was "very similar" or "quite similar" to the tests included in textbooks—tests which, as we have seen, teachers use frequently.[13]

But it is external tests that have increasingly driven what is taught in schools. And this is no accident. As part of their attempt to hold schools accountable for student performance, states and school districts have not only implemented testing programs but have also made sure that there are consequences—real or perceived—attached to the results. That way, students and schools have an incentive to keep their "eyes on the prize" and to improve performance. Thus in recent years a growing number of states have made sure that good things happen to schools where test scores go up and (in some cases) bad things happen when they go down. As we will see, these policies have had the desired effect of making teachers and schools pay attention to the tests and strive to boost scores, but these efforts have not always ended up the way public officials intended.

The most common method by which districts have placed high stakes on the test results is simply publicizing them. Just as teachers regularly send report cards to parents to show individual student progress, some states and school districts have created report cards to show the performance of schools. The idea is the same: parents are expected to reward high-performing schools and put pressure on low-performing schools to improve, just as they reward their children for doing well and urge them to buckle down when they need improvement.

Sometimes the pressure exerted through public reporting is less subtle. When he became superintendent of the Prince George's County, Maryland, school district outside of Washington, D.C., John A. Murphy pledged to raise the average test score in the district to the seventy-fifth percentile and to reduce the gap between the scores of whites and blacks. He carried out this pledge by removing student artwork that had graced the walls of the conference room adjacent to his office and replacing it with charts that showed the test performance of every school in the district, along with the principal's name. Principals summoned to the conference room—known as the "applied anxiety room"—quickly got the message, and test scores went up (although they fell again when the state changed the test it used).

The federal government has also tried its hand at creating a report card for the states; that effort, too, proved hotly controversial. Beginning in 1984, the year after *The Nation at Risk* was released, Secretary Bell annually released a "wall chart" that attempted to show how the fifty states ranked in education performance. The factors he used to measure state performance were dropout rates and average scores on the two major college admissions tests: the Scholastic Aptitude Test and the American College Testing program test.

State officials (and the companies that produced the tests) immediately criticized the use of the test scores to rank states as misleading and unfair. They argued that since students volunteered to take the tests—only those planning to attend colleges that required the tests for admission elected to take the SAT or the ACT—the average scores did not reflect a true measure of average student performance in the state. If the characteristics of the students who chose to take the tests changed, the average score might go up or down, but this change would have nothing to do with the quality of education in the state. Moreover, the argument continued, the tests themselves did not measure a state's education program, since they were designed to be "common yardsticks" to measure students' abilities regardless of where students attended school.

Despite these arguments, Secretary Bell and his successors, William Bennett and Lauro F. Cavazos, persisted in releasing the wall chart each year. Recognizing the handwriting on the wall chart, the Council of Chief State School Officers reversed decades of policy and agreed by a margin of one vote to endorse a new way of comparing student achievement across states. That decision helped lend support for the expansion of NAEP, which, unlike the SAT and the ACT, is administered to a representative sample of students and measures achievement in subject areas, not just generic skills.

State and federal officials in 1991 created a new national report card to show state and national progress toward the six national education goals set by President George Bush and the nation's governors. The first goals report included states' performance on NAEP as information on progress toward the goal of ensuring that all students "demonstrate competency in challenging subject matter." Following the institution of the goals report, Secretary of Education Lamar Alexander quietly dropped the wall chart.

Like the state and school district officials before them, the governors and Bush Administration officials on the National Education Goals Panel portrayed their attempt to provide a report card on education performance as a "wake-up call" to arouse a complacent citizenry into action to raise performance. But it is unclear whether the goals report or any of the school report cards have produced the desired effects. For one thing, the reports have tended to generate little attention outside a relatively small group of committed and informed citizens and professionals. (With one exception: real-estate agents often snatch up the report cards and use school test scores as selling points for homes neighboring high-scoring schools.)

The report cards have also failed to answer the question of what citizens and parents are supposed to do once they have information about a school's performance. One action that parents can take in a number of states is to send their children to another school. At least a dozen states allow parents some form of choice among public schools in the state. But there is little evidence that parents who take advantage of this option use report cards about school performance to make their decisions. In Minnesota, the first state to open enrollment in every school, Rudy Perpich, as governor, proposed a statewide testing program to provide "consumer information" about the quality of schools in the state, but that proposal was rejected by the legislature. Despite their limited impact on the public, the report cards have succeeded in one respect, though: they have made schools place even greater emphasis on the tests. Whether or not parents pay any attention or take any action, principals want to make sure that their school looks good when the test scores are published in newspapers, and they encourage teachers to take steps to see that scores go up. "What gets measured gets taught," a report by the Southern Regional Education Board notes. "What gets reported gets taught twice as well."[14]

In addition to reporting the results publicly, states and school districts have also raised the stakes on tests by attaching consequences to the results—rewarding success and punishing failure. About half the math teachers in the Boston College survey responded that the achievement tests were "extremely important" or "very important" in student placement and in administrators' evaluations of schools and school districts.[15]

In some cases, students themselves have been held accountable for performance. Seventeen of the thirty-six states with minimum-competency tests, for example, tie grade-to-grade promotion or high school graduation (or both) directly to a test. If students pass the test, they can cross the threshold; if not, they have to wait until they do pass. The use of tests as promotional gates received a significant boost in 1983, when the Florida Supreme Court ruled that the state could legally withhold a diploma from a student who failed to pass a basic-skills test as long as the student was taught what the test measured.

Two states even erected tests as gates to entry into school. In Georgia and Mississippi, legislatures approved policies to test kindergartners to determine whether they were ready to enter the first grade. In Georgia, for example, every child in kindergarten had to pass a ninety-minute achievement test and a teacher's evaluation in order to advance to first grade; any child who failed to was placed in a "transitional" class. But these tests drew sharp criticism from educators and children's advocates, who contended that the tests were poor measures of young children's abilities and could unfairly exclude from school many children who could do well. Faced with such opposition, the legislatures reversed themselves and dropped the kindergarten tests.

Some of the state testing programs have offered rewards for high performance. For more than a century, New York State has offered Regents Examinations, which test students at the end of high school courses. Students who elect to take the exams and pass them are eligible for a special diploma, known as a Regents diploma. California in 1983 adopted a similar program, known as Golden State Examinations.

California also briefly experimented with a program to provide cash awards for students who perform well on the regular state testing program, the California Assessment Program. The "cash for CAP" program, later dropped for budget reasons, was explicitly aimed at offering an incentive for students to perform, as state officials explained: "The majority of students are not working up to their potential, and . . . it is the responsibility of the schools to challenge them to do so—both for their own good and for the good of society."[16]

Other states, meanwhile, have chosen to focus on school performance. At least seven states have adopted programs to reward schools that demonstrate high levels of student performance, in most cases by providing cash awards. South Carolina, though, tried an unusual twist to this idea. Schools where test scores show significant improvement are free from many state regulations, such as those governing the number of minutes of instruction for each subject each day. Educators in South Carolina say the deregulation program provides an incentive for schools to keep their test scores up, if only so they can maintain their status as a special school.

A more controversial (and thus less common) strategy is punishing failing schools. The first state to adopt this approach was New Jersey, which used its new authority by taking over the "academically bankrupt" Jersey City school district. But while lagging test scores were only one of many factors that led to the takeover there, officials in other states with similar programs, notably South Carolina, suggest that the threat of possible takeover has motivated schools to improve test performance.

The explosion in testing, particularly high-stakes testing, over the past two decades has put enormous weight on tests and has placed them squarely in the center of schooling. Now teachers as well as students are asking, "Will this be on the test?"

But the emphasis on tests has raised serious questions: Do increases in test scores truly reflect increases in student achievement? Are schools focusing on material tested to the exclusion of other knowledge and skills that may be important? Do the types of tests schools use measure all of the abilities students must be able to demonstrate?

Increasingly, educators are answering no to all of these questions. Educators and researchers have amassed evidence of significant problems with the growing reliance on tests, confirming suspicions that teachers since Horace Mann's time have held: namely, that using tests as gauges of teacher or school performance is unfair. Faced with such evidence, and adding their own as well, schools such as Littleton have begun their search for alternatives.

In the next chapter, we will consider the criticism of traditional tests and look at the growing demands for new measures that might more accurately reflect, and indeed enhance, student learning.

Chapter Three

The Emperor Has No Clothes

John Jacob Cannell was practicing family medicine in the small town of Beaver, West Virginia, in 1987 when he began noticing something strange. The children he was seeing in his clinic appeared deeply troubled, yet when he asked their schools about them, he was told that they were all performing "above average."

Checking further, Cannell learned that the school district overall was above average, a finding that to him did not make sense: If this poor Appalachian town was above average, he asked himself, what place could possibly be below average? To find out, he surveyed the states and large cities to learn their test scores. His results, published in a small pamphlet out of his house, catapulted the country doctor into the national spotlight and rocked the foundations of the testing enterprise in the United States.

Cannell found that, contrary to what appeared to be common sense, every state and most cities reported that the average test score of their elementary school students was "above the national average." This finding soon became known as the "Lake Wobegon® effect," after the humorist Garrison Keillor's fictional town, where "all the women are strong, all the men are good-looking, and all the children are above average."[1]

Though Cannell's methods were flawed and he overstated his case, his study helped expose many of the problems brought on by the explosion of high-stakes testing in schools and cast a heavy shadow of doubt on the tests and the way they were used. Like the boy in the story who dared to reveal that the emperor had no clothes, the West Virginia physician showed that tests did not do what they were supposed to do: inform people about the state of student achievement.

To the general public, Cannell's finding appeared to defy logic, and it led many people to wonder whether school officials were misleading them in reporting test scores. To those familiar with testing, the finding—confirmed by a federally sponsored study by leading experts—pointed up many of the problems brought on by reliance on high-stakes testing. In any event, Cannell's small, crude study helped fuel a mounting criticism of the enterprise.

Criticism of tests is nothing new, of course. Almost from the outset, tests have come under fire for misjudging people's abilities and acting as inappropriate "gate-keepers" to advancement. As Stephen Jay Gould writes in *The Mismeasure of Man*, measures of human intelligence have always reached the same conclusion: that those doing the testing are superior to those from other, less privileged racial and ethnic groups. And the disadvantaged groups have suffered in the process.[2]

But while a few writers, notably Walter Lippman, raised their voices in protest against increased testing as it advanced, they were not able to stem the testing tide; as we have seen, it has engulfed schools throughout this century. In the past decade, though, the critics have grown more vocal. Such groups as the National Center for Fair & Open Testing (known as FairTest), an organization started by the consumer advocate Ralph Nader, have accused tests of bias against girls and members of minority groups, claiming that they fail to take into account the diverse cultural backgrounds or problem-solving styles of test-takers. Critics have also argued, successfully in some cases, that tests are inappropriate for very young children, since the results do not reliably reflect their abilities.

By the time Cannell released his pamphlet in the fall of 1987, the chorus of criticism of the use of high-stakes testing in schools had grown quite loud, as had the emerging chorus calling for alternatives to traditional tests. And as a big man with a booming baritone voice, Cannell was able to make himself heard from statehouses to the corridors of the U.S. Education Department, where officials held a high-level meeting in early 1988 to examine his findings.

Interpreting Norm-Referenced Scores

The phenomenon Cannell identified in his report came about because of a little-known but key feature of the way standardized tests are designed. Contrary to many parents' assumptions, a child's score on a test—whether "above the national average" or "in the seventy-fifth percentile"—is not based on a comparison with the other students who took the test that year. If that were the case, then only half the test-takers could indeed be above average. Rather, the test scores are based on comparisons with a "norm group" of children—a group that may have taken the test as many as seven years before.

When test publishers produce a new version of a test, they first administer it to a representative sample of students across the nation. Their scores become the "national norms" against which all subsequent scores are compared. Publishers also produce norms for different groups of students (such as urban students and those who attend independent schools) for schools that wish to compare their students' performance with that of students from like schools. Publishers usually cannot base their norms on the tests they sell, since the students who take their tests are not a representative sample of all students in the nation.

Norming is an important feature of testing. As H. D. Hoover, the director of the Iowa Basic Skills Testing Program, explains, norms place test scores in context much the way they place information about size in context. Without norms, the statement, "He is six feet tall and weighs 100 pounds" is meaningless for comparison; knowing roughly what the average weight for someone that tall is, however, we can say, "He is thin."

But despite that advantage, norming also poses a number of problems. For one thing, norm-referenced scores provide a very limited view of what students know and can do. Presenting a student's performance only in comparison to that of other students says little about the skills and knowledge a student has attained. A score does not indicate which questions a student answered correctly and which she answered incorrectly; indeed, because students need only *choose* an answer, not construct it, we do not know whether they possess the knowledge and skills the question was designed to tap or simply guessed well.

This problem is made worse by the fact that conventional tests are kept secret. In order to prevent students from seeing the questions in advance, test publishers and schools have devised elaborate security procedures. But the effect of these measures is to hide from students and their parents the knowledge and skills the students are expected to demonstrate and to hide from students and teachers their corrected work. All they get back is a score. That score may indicate that a student performed better than average, but better than average on what?

As a result of this limitation, teachers say they seldom find norm-referenced tests useful for diagnosing students' strengths and weaknesses. In a study conducted in Pennsylvania, for example, teachers said tests only *supplement* what they already know about their students. If classroom performance and test scores diverge, teachers give their own observations more credence.[3]

A second problem with norm-referenced tests is related to the first. Even if a student performed in the seventy-fifth percentile—that is, better than three-fourths of the norm group—we do not know how good that is. What if the norm group consisted of poor performers? This problem becomes particularly serious when scores are reported in terms of grade levels, as they often are. If a student's score is at "3.2," for example, that means she performed at about the average of those in the second month of third grade. But this score is less informative than one might think. We do not know whether the third-graders are doing single-digit arithmetic or calculus.

In the past few years, as we will see, educators and public officials have been sitting down to determine what all students should know and be able to do in key subjects. When completed, these efforts will become the first national standards for student performance. But in the absence of such standards, each local school board—and in many cases, local school—can largely decide for itself what its curriculum and goals for student achievement should be. Many educators believe this is as it should be: a community of teachers, parents, and school administrators should determine what students should know and be able to do. But in fact, few schools actually do so. Without setting goals for student performance, many simply rely on textbooks to define the curriculum and to provide tests to measure progress on it.

But even if schools set their own goals, they have no way to compare students against the goals; simply reviewing their students' scores on standardized tests is clearly not sufficient. Another problem with norm-referenced test scores is the problem that Cannell identified. Because most publishers set norms only about once every seven years—it is too costly to do it more often, they say—schools' test scores can rise each year while the norms stay the same. The result: everybody can be above average. Although testing experts criticized Cannell for his methodology, a subsequent study by Robert L. Linn and his colleagues at the University of Colorado, Boulder, confirmed that almost all states and most school districts reported test results above the national average.[4]

Test publishers, who reacted strongly to Cannell's charges, pointed out that this result may reflect genuine improvements in student achievement. In fact, evidence from the publishers' own norming studies and from other sources suggests that achievement did rise during the 1980s; thus student performance at the time of Cannell's study *should* have been above that of the average of the norm group. Results from the National Assessment of Educational Progress, for example, show that the average mathematics performance of U.S. students improved substantially during the 1980s. The average performance of nine-year-olds in 1990 was significantly higher than that in any previous assessment, while that of thirteen-year-olds was higher than their performance a decade earlier. Seventeen-year-olds, meanwhile, whose math performance declined in the 1970s, showed significant progress between 1982 and 1990.

In reading, by contrast, the results were more mixed, but the National Assessment showed that the reading performance of seventeen-year-olds was significantly higher in 1990 than it was in 1975.[5]

Despite those findings, there is also considerable evidence that the test scores Cannell reported were inflated and showed greater improvement than in fact occurred. Moreover, this inflation was a direct result of the high stakes this country placed on the tests. We are faced with a paradox: states and school districts imposed testing mandates on schools and put consequences on the results to make sure that schools improved, but these actions only ensured that we could not see the true picture of student performance.

To Cannell, the high test scores reflected flagrant cheating. Because schools used the same tests year after year, he alleged, the teachers and principals knew the questions and answers and could feed them to students or even change their answer sheets. As evidence, he noted that several states that had elaborate procedures to ensure test security—such as California and Maine—had lower rates of test-score increases.

This charge lent an air of sensationalism to Cannell's already provocative findings and helped attract even more publicity for them. He appeared on an episode of 60 Minutes entitled "Teacher Is a Cheater," which also focused on a case involving a South Carolina teacher who was charged with violating state law by changing students' answer sheets on statewide tests. Following that television appearance, Cannell began receiving letters from other teachers around the country confessing their own misdeeds or charging others with committing similar ones.

Cheating certainly exists in schools, and there is little doubt that the pressure to boost test scores might induce otherwise honest students and educators to consider it. The California Department of Education found dozens of incidents in which answer sheets on the California Assessment Program had been altered. And the *Wall Street Journal* in 1992 published a long article that alleged widespread cheating at one of Pittsburgh's most prestigious high schools. Despite those cases, though, there is little evidence that cheating is epidemic in schools or that such practices are the reason test scores have risen.[6]

Nevertheless, there is considerable evidence that educators have not been above employing some questionable practices to make sure test scores go up. One of these practices is retaining low-achieving students in their grades. Though researchers have documented the harm to students in holding them back for another year—students who are over the age of their classmates are much more likely than others to drop out of school, for example—many parents and policy makers continue to favor the practice to curb "social promotion" and to provide extra help for students who appear to be falling behind in their schoolwork. But grade retention also has the effect of boosting average test scores. Here is an example: if a school district tests third-graders, a school that retains its lowest performers in second grade for an additional year will have fewer low performers taking the third-grade test. And when the low performers eventually get into third grade, they will have had the benefit of an additional year of second-grade work and may do better on the test than they otherwise would have done.

A study by researchers from the State University of New York, Albany, found some evidence that grade retention had produced this effect on test scores. The researchers looked at two schools that were basically alike, except that one retained about 5 percent of its students from kindergarten through grade two while the other retained about 25 percent of its students in those years. The school with the higher retention rate, the researchers found, had won numerous awards, partly on the basis of its high third-grade test scores.

The researchers also found that, in addition to retaining students, some schools may classify low-achieving students as learning disabled in order to exclude them from mandated tests and boost their average scores. In most states, students with disabilities are exempt from testing requirements or are given tests under special conditions, in which case their scores do not count toward a school's average.

The Albany researchers quote one elementary school principal who admitted that he opted to exclude low performers from the test rather than give them additional help:

> We have that third grade test that we have to deal with. So we either have to exempt the kid from taking the basic skills test through special ed or get him ready to take that test. . . .
>
> There may be a kid who is [learning disabled] but the LD teacher and the classroom teacher think this kid could be able to take the test. Now I have a problem with that. . . . They don't real-ize that my neck is on the block if they take the test and fail it. So I want them exempted. So what I say to the second grade teachers, "Any kid you have that is LD and you think is probably going to fail that test, I want him exempted."[7]

"Teaching to the Test"

More commonly, school administrators and teachers have sought to raise test scores through various practices known as "teaching to the test." Teaching to the test is often frowned upon in schools, but it is not necessarily a bad thing. Different tests measure different knowledge and skills, and administrators usually select the test that most closely matches a school's curriculum. They want their teach-ers to emphasize the skills and knowledge the test measures because those are the skills and knowledge they think are important. In a survey of officials in forty states with high-stakes testing programs, Lorrie A. Shepard, a professor of education at the University of Col-orado, Boulder, found near-unanimous agreement that teachers spend more time teaching skills and knowledge they know to be objectives of a required test than they spend teaching other skills and knowledge. As one official responded, "In fact, the presence of the test is forcing attention to the essential skills that had been identified."[8]

Some educators have argued that this is an appropriate function of tests. Since teachers pay attention to tests, why not use tests to inspire improvements in instruction?

In practice, though, teaching to the test has distorted the information tests provide about what students know and the way teachers teach. And it has become more and more common as states and school districts have imposed testing mandates and used test scores to hold schools accountable for student performance.

As a number of researchers have noted, the term "teaching to the test" actually covers a range of activities, some of which are clearly unethical. On the unethical side of the spectrum are practices such as giving students actual test questions or answers. But other techniques teachers use to prepare students for tests are quite benign. For example, many schools hold pep rallies the day before tests to encourage students to do well. And one school in Pennsylvania tried to motivate students to do well on the tests by broadcasting over the loudspeaker this song, sung to the tune of "High Hopes":

> We have worked and studied so long,
> Hope we don't get anything wrong,
> As you have probably guessed
> On the test
> We'll do our very best
> 'Cause we've got high hopes. . . .[9]

In between those two extremes are a number of practices that raise questions about the tests and their influence on instruction. As Lorrie Shepard found in her survey of state officials, many schools use practice tests to familiarize students with the format and type of questions used on the test. This is reasonable; it would be unfair to spring a multiple-choice test on a youngster who had never answered that sort of question before. Some practice tests, though, include questions that are very similar to those used in commercially available standardized achievement tests. "One-time practice with test format, especially when these activities are consistent with standardization procedures, is not the cause of inflated test scores," Shepard writes. "However, repeated practice or instruction geared to the format of the test rather than the content domain can increase scores without increasing achievement."[10]

One survey of math and science teachers suggests that such test-preparation practices are more common in predominantly minority classrooms. Among classes where more than 60 percent of the students were members of minority groups, the survey found, about three-fourths of teachers reported teaching test-taking skills and beginning test preparation more than a month before the test. In classes with few minority students, by contrast, about 40 percent of teachers said they employed such practices. Likewise, a separate survey of upper-elementary teachers found that those with more disadvantaged students were twice as likely as those teaching wealthier students to report giving practice tests and practicing with old versions of mandated standardized tests.[11]

Another problem with teaching to the test is that it can narrow the curriculum to the material on the test. There are only so many hours in a school day; teachers who choose to focus on what is tested must leave something else out. In some extreme cases, whole subject areas are left out, at least for part of the year. If the state tests students in reading and mathematics, for example, teachers may put off instruction in science and social studies until after the test.

One example of this practice comes from Maryland, where the state requires students to pass "functional" (or basic-skills) tests in reading, writing, mathematics, and citizenship in order to graduate from high school. The citizenship test, in particular, proved difficult for many students, who found the detailed questions about local, state, and federal governments daunting. As a result, teachers there spent time teaching about civics at the expense of other subjects. As one building administrator said, "We realize a kid is taken out of science every other day for citizenship and will fail science to maybe pass the citizenship test."[12]

In other cases, schools resort to the absurd practice of "doubling up" the curriculum in order to teach both what is on the test and what they want to teach. The Pelham Road Elementary School in Greenville, South Carolina, for example, has automated its library and has begun to instruct students in how to scroll through computers to find the materials they need. Teachers there consider this an important skill, since many public and research libraries have also moved to computerized systems. But since the state testing program tests students on their ability to use traditional card catalogues, the school has also maintained its card catalogue and teaches students to use it as well, thus spending valuable curricular time on a skill the school has determined is outmoded.

More frequently, teaching the content tested means teaching a narrow segment of a subject area. As Lee Cronbach, one of the leading scholars in the field, noted three decades ago, no test can measure all of the knowledge and skills in a whole subject. As he stated, "Whenever it is critically important to master certain content, the knowledge that it will be tested produces a desirable concentration of effort. On the other hand, learning the answer to a set of questions is by no means the same as acquiring understanding of whatever topic that question represents."[13]

As with the previously cited features of teaching to the test, narrowing instruction to the material on standardized tests has a disturbing characteristic: it appears to be more prevalent in low-income and minority classes than it does in schools that cater to more affluent students. According to one survey, disadvantaged students are less likely than their more affluent peers to receive instruction in science, art, thinking skills, and other areas not included on standardized tests.[14] Thus tests drive instruction more for minorities, who tend to lag behind whites in test performance. Perhaps schools make more of a deliberate effort to teach to the tests with students who seem to be falling behind. Perhaps teachers in predominantly white schools feel they do not need to take special steps to raise scores, since their students perform well on the tests anyway.

But, in practice, the emphasis on raising test scores has thrown into doubt the meaning of the higher test scores. If test scores go up because schools have focused extensively on preparing students for the test at the expense of other material, what does the increase signify? To cite one commonly used analogy, placing all your energy on raising test scores is like prescribing massive doses of aspirin to lower the fever of a cancer patient. You may succeed in reducing her fever, but you have not addressed the underlying problem.

A detailed study of one urban school district found concrete evidence that suggests that schools' emphasis on raising test scores masks the true level of achievement of their students. Examining a group of third-graders, Daniel M. Koretz and his colleagues at the National Center for Research on Evaluation, Standards, and Student Testing found that the students performed much worse on tests they had not seen before than they did on their district's tests, even though the tests measured the same general content and skills. In math, the difference in the average performance on the test was as much as eight academic months—in other words, the district's test suggested that the third-graders were nearly a year ahead of where the new test suggested they were in math. The difference in reading performance was smaller but still significant.[15]

In addition to corrupting the information from test results, focusing on raising test performance has adversely affected student learning. It is increasingly clear that the standardized achievement tests in place in most schools do not measure what educators and the public think is important, and the heavy emphasis on teaching the material on the tests has steered instruction away from what is necessary.

In the past few years, teachers in a number of disciplines have begun to spell out, for the first time, what they believe all students ought to know and be able to do. These efforts represent a radical departure for American education. They are based on the idea that all students can learn at high levels. But in representing that view, these standards for student performance stand in sharp contrast to the type of abilities tests tend to measure. For example, the National Council of Teachers of Mathematics has outlined standards for school mathematics that call for less emphasis on paper-and-pencil calculations and more on enabling students to use their mathematical knowledge to solve real-world problems and to communicate their reasoning. The standards also urge an increased focus on topics seldom taught in schools (such as statistics), particularly in the early grades.[16]

A study by the Boston College Center for the Study of Testing, Evaluation, and Educational Policy provides the most compelling evidence of the mismatch between teachers' goals and test content. Analyzing the six major standardized tests, as well as the tests included in the four major textbooks and textbook series in math and science, the researchers found that the tests did not tap the higher-level skills and content educators consider vital. In particular, the study found that 40 percent of the items on the standardized math tests asked students to perform simple computations, and more than two-thirds of the items tested basic arithmetic operations. By contrast, only 3 percent of the items on both the standardized and textbook tests measured high-level conceptual knowledge, and about 5 percent tested higher-level thinking skills, such as the ability to formulate and solve problems and to demonstrate reasoning and communication.

In science, the picture was only somewhat different. Less than one-fourth of the science items called for high-level conceptual work, and less than 10 percent asked students to design, execute, interpret, and evaluate experiments.[17]

Test publishers responding to the study charged that it was out of date and that newer versions of tests more closely reflect the goals of the math and science reformers. And they may be right. After all, multiple-choice tests *can* tap high-level reasoning and problem-solving skills.

In practice, though, these newer versions of the standardized tests have yet to enter widespread use. Because of the strong influence of tests on instruction, it is not surprising that students have learned basic computation and factual recall and not problem solving and comprehension. Data from the National Assessment of Educational Progress bear this out. NAEP found, in a 1990 reading test, that nearly all middle school and high school students showed a basic understanding of stories and the ability to summarize main ideas and to distill information from the material present. But only 11 percent of thirteen-year-olds could read and comprehend a wide variety of text materials and elaborate on the information and ideas presented. And only 7 percent of seventeen-year-olds—students about to enter higher education or the workforce—could understand specialized content or grasp the meaning of passages that contained challenging material.

Similarly, in math NAEP found that virtually all students knew simple arithmetic facts and that 82 percent of nine-year-olds and all of the older students showed an understanding of two-digit numbers and could read charts and graphs. Only 17 percent of the thirteen-year-olds, however, could compute with decimals, simple fractions, and commonly used percents, and only 7 percent of the seventeen-year-olds demonstrated an understanding of multistep problem solving and algebra.[18]

To some, these findings are a sign of success. The minimum-competency testing movement was aimed at ensuring that all students would attain a level of basic skills, and it worked. We want to know if students have mastered the basic skills, and multiple-choice tests are an efficient way to find out if they have done so.

But to others, the NAEP data present an ominous trend and suggest that the "minimum competency" the tests demand has become the maximum that schools expect. In the absence of clear, high standards for student performance, some schools have allowed the basic-skills tests to dictate what should be taught. In a prescient 1984 article, Norman Frederiksen of the Educational Testing Service called this influence of tests on instruction, not the alleged discrimination against women and minorities, "the real test bias." Frederiksen writes,

> Improvement in basic skills is of course much to be desired, and the use of tests to achieve that outcome is not to be condemned. My concern, however, is that reliance on objective tests to provide evidence of improvement may have contributed to a bias in education that decreases effort to teach other important abilities that are difficult to measure with multiple-choice tests. . . . [T]he possibility must be considered that the mandated use of minimum-competency tests, which use the multiple-choice format almost exclusively, may have discouraged the teaching of abilities that cannot easily be measured with multiple-choice items.[19]

The "Thinking Curriculum"

How do we know that these so-called higher-level abilities are important for all students? One answer comes from the American economy. In the not-too-distant past, most people could rely on basic skills. Workers stayed in one job for most of their lives, and companies were structured so that the few, the managers, made most of the decisions, and the many, the line workers, followed through on them, doing largely routine tasks.

Increasingly, that pattern no longer holds. Workers now change their jobs half a dozen times throughout their work lives, meaning that they need the ability to learn and to adapt to new environments. At the same time, the old hierarchical structures are breaking down in many companies. In these workplaces, everyone from the shop floor to the corporate suite makes decisions, so everyone needs to be able to analyze evidence, solve problems, and communicate. New skills as well, such as the ability to work in teams, are at a premium.

In perhaps a more important sense, the idea that higher-level skills and knowledge are essential for all also comes from a substantial body of knowledge that over the past quarter-century has transformed our understanding of how children learn. By studying the way young people think and the way teachers teach, scientists have found that the way classrooms are currently organized—in particular, the use of tests—is misguided; and they have proposed alternatives that would enhance, not impede, learning.

The traditional theory of education, which holds sway in most classrooms today, is based on behavioral psychology. In that view, a subject area is broken down into its component skills and knowledge, and students progress through it sequentially, moving on to more complex skills after they have mastered the basics.

Scientists involved in the "cognitive revolution," however, have found that learning even elementary tasks involves complex thinking and reasoning. Thus, as noted earlier, Lauren Resnick has argued that the entire school curriculum should be a "thinking curriculum" and that so-called higher-order skills, once reserved for the few, should be taught to all students.

The research that has led to this new way of thinking about thinking comes from a wide range of fields, including computer science, linguistics, psychology, and sociology. Cognitive scientists challenging the traditional view of learning as a one-way path from teacher to student have found that children actively "construct" knowledge based on what they already know and through interactions with their environment.

Thus teaching abstract concepts, in isolation from the real world, does not help children learn and may in fact keep them from learning. But that is what schools do. Researchers have found, for example, that children in all parts of the world have a highly developed sense of mathematical concepts such as "number." They know, from observing the world, that if they add something to something else, they will have more of it. Studies of illiterate street vendors in Brazil, for example, showed that these unschooled youths could make complex calculations rapidly. Schools, however, act as if such knowledge and abilities do not exist. They begin teaching mathematics, with its formal symbols, as an abstract language that has little connection to the world students know. Students who learn math that way learn it as a series of rules they must follow, not as a way of understanding the world. In one widely cited instance, students were asked to determine how many buses an army would need to transport a group of soldiers. Having been told that a bus holds forty people, the students followed the rule and came out with an answer that included a fraction, without realizing that such an answer is absurd.[20]

Sometimes children's knowledge of the world is wrong, and if schools fail to acknowledge and correct the misconceptions, students may emerge from schooling with them intact. In a recent book, *The Unschooled Mind,* the Harvard University psychologist Howard Gardner argues that even "well-educated" college graduates can think like five-year-olds and believe that the earth's distance from the sun, not the tilt on its axis, causes the seasons, if schooling does not connect them with the real world.[21]

Cognitive research has also challenged the view that the acquisition of skills and knowledge takes place sequentially, through a set of increasingly complex skills. By studying experts and novices in a range of subject areas, scientists have found that skilled readers, mathematicians, scientists, and writers are not just more advanced than beginners. Rather, they approach their tasks differently. And they are aware of their thinking processes, through the concept known as "metacognition."

In reading, for example, studies have shown that understanding even simple passages demands a large set of complex skills and knowledge. By following the eye movements of skilled readers, scientists have found that readers are constantly "making meaning" of a text. They not only decode words; they also stop to "process" them into clauses and sentences and to think about what comes next. Scientists have also found that readers, in order to make inferences and retain what they have read, require background knowledge.

For children to learn in ways that promote understanding, teachers must provide opportunities for students to demonstrate their abilities through performances—graphically or through written or oral presentations, for example. To David N. Perkins, a professor of education at Harvard University, performance is the essence of understanding. A student may have a vast storehouse of knowledge about a topic. But if she cannot explain the topic—generate analogies, muster evidence in support of her explanations—on a range of performances, then she does not truly understand it. "All performances can be called performances of understanding," Perkins says. "They are the earmarks of what it is to understand something."[22]

The findings from cognitive science have profound implications for schools and particularly for testing. Not only do the tests used in schools focus almost exclusively on basic skills, as the Boston College study found, but the tests themselves, by their very design, are fundamentally flawed and cannot allow students to demonstrate what they know and are able to do. We need a new way.

In a 1992 article, Lauren Resnick and Daniel Resnick outline two key assumptions of tests that they say are incompatible with the goals of a thinking curriculum. First, they point out, the tests are based on the idea that we can break down a skill such as reading into component parts and measure students' abilities on each part. Tests of reading comprehension, for example, tend to present short passages and pose a series of questions that ask students to recall facts from the passages or to identify interpretations of them, not to show their own understanding. "Under these conditions," the Resnicks write, "reading comprehension appears to be a matter of finding predetermined answers, not interpreting the written word."

The second erroneous assumption of tests is the idea that knowledge can be taken out of the context in which it is applied. As an example, the Resnicks note that tests measure students' language-usage ability—an important part of writing ability—in isolation, rather than as an essential aspect of composition. They ask students to find a spelling error in a list of words or to identify the predicate adjective in a sentence, for example. Students who practice the type of language-usage exercises included on such tests, the Resnicks say, might become good copyeditors, but they would not become good writers.[23]

Howard Gardner, who pioneered the idea of "multiple intelligences," adds that tests are flawed for another reason: they fail to capture the diverse abilities of young people. Gardner's research, based on studies of young children and brain-damaged adults, challenges the traditional view of intelligence as a single dimension that paper-and-pencil tests can measure. Rather, Gardner argues, people have several "intelligences" that do not all develop at the same rate. Children, for example, can appear highly skilled in one or two areas but not in others; adults suffering from brain damage, meanwhile, can lose some brain functions but otherwise appear competent.

Gardner argues that there are, in fact, at least seven autonomous intelligences: linguistic intelligence, such as that exhibited by a poet; logical-mathematical intelligence, which scientists employ; musical intelligence; spatial intelligence, useful for painters, sailors, and architects; bodily-kinesthetic intelligence, common to athletes and actors; interpersonal intelligence, encompassing the knowledge of others used by salespeople and politicians; and intrapersonal intelligence, which is knowledge of oneself. These intelligences are potentials; usually, honing the skills each involves requires instruction and practice. But schools and achievement tests measure only the first two.

Working along a parallel track, Robert J. Sternberg, the Yale University psychologist, has proposed a "triarchic" theory of intelligence. In addition to the analytic intelligence that tests measure, Sternberg would add creative intelligence, which enables people to confront new situations, and practical intelligence, which enables them to apply what they know to everyday circumstances.[24]

Pursuing a corollary of these ideas, the Resnicks, Gardner, and Sternberg have argued, with other researchers, for new forms of student assessment that would more accurately gauge student abilities. Moreover, teaching to these alternative assessments is the kind of instruction that would lead to complex thinking. As the Resnicks state, you get what you assess, and you do not get what you do not assess. Therefore, we should build assessments toward which we want educators to teach. The Resnicks conclude: "Assessments must be designed so that when teachers do the natural thing—that is, prepare their students to perform well—they will exercise the kinds of abilities and develop the kinds of skills and knowledge that are the real goals of education reform. This principle assumes that what is in the assessment will be practiced in the classroom, in a form close to the assessment form. For any proposed assessment exercise, it directs us to pose one central question: 'Is this what we want students to be doing with their instructional time?'"[25]

The Quest for Alternatives

As alternatives to traditional tests, the reformers endorse methods that fall generally into three categories: performance-based assessments, projects, and portfolios. While these methods of measuring student performance are not completely new—they have been tried in classrooms and in research settings for many years—they do represent a substantial departure for most schools, particularly when applied to the external testing that has increasingly influenced instructional practice and the public's view of schooling. We will see specific examples of these new instruments in the next chapter. But their basic principles are as follows:

- *Performance-based assessments* are exercises that ask students to demonstrate their knowledge and skills by undertaking some type of performance, such as writing an essay or conducting a science experiment. Such requirements are common in athletics and the arts. Divers, for example, demonstrate their abilities by diving, not by answering written questions about techniques. Similarly, pianists are judged on their ability to play a Chopin étude.

- In contrast to performances, which can be relatively short in duration, *projects* are extended exercises that ask students to generate problems, come up with solutions, and then demonstrate their findings. One analogy is the type of activity Boy and Girl Scouts undertake to earn merit badges. Scouts on a camping trip, for example, must show that they can plan and execute the trip as well as deal with all of the unexpected situations that arise.

- *Portfolios* are long-term records of a student's performances. These are commonly used by artists and photographers to show gallery owners and editors the range of their work and their development over time.

All of these types of assessments share features that researchers and educators have advocated to counteract some of the negative aspects of conventional tests. Unlike the traditional tests, the new assessments match the type of instruction that cognitive scientists say enhances learning. For one thing, in place of abstract exercises cooked up just for the test, the new assessments demand work in a real-world context. For this reason, alternative assessments are often called *authentic* assessments.

In carrying out a project—for example, preparing a videotape on the origins of the Civil War—a student must act like a documentary producer. He must gather information, sift through it, formulate a thesis, weigh the evidence for and against the thesis, write a script, and present his videotape. He is actively constructing his knowledge and skills, not receiving knowledge passively and in abstract form, the way students do when they hear lectures on the Civil War and then answer test questions based on the lectures. At the same time, if the videotape project is more meaningful to the student than a lecture-based test, he may find himself more motivated to do well on the assessment.

The new forms of assessments also allow students to demonstrate complex thinking, not just isolated skills. The student preparing the videotape must analyze and weigh facts, not just recall them. He must write something that marshals evidence in support of a conclusion. These assessments also challenge the view, implicit in multiple-choice tests, that there is only one right answer to every question and that the goal is to find it and to find it quickly. There may be more than one way to interpret a poem or a historical event. And, as in real life, the most important goal may be coming up with ways to find answers. Moreover, these assessments teach students that it takes time to solve complex problems. Students trained to answer long series of multiple-choice questions come to believe that if they cannot solve a problem within a few minutes, they will be unable to solve it at all. We want them to use their creativity and hard work to solve problems, just as we want them to on the job and in life.

Often these alternative assessments bring other skills to bear as well. Some require students to collaborate to solve a problem. Others allow students to show their metacognitive skills by identifying how they made a particular decision.

The new assessments also permit students to demonstrate a range of abilities. The videotape assessment, for example, taps a number of Howard Gardner's intelligence categories: spatial intelligence, required as students design a set; interpersonal intelligence, required as students interview; logical-mathematical intelligence, required as students develop an argument; and linguistic intelligence, required as students attempt to present that argument effectively.

Finally, the new assessments are judged differently from conventional tests. Although they can be used to compare students, the primary goal is to see if students demonstrate certain abilities. Like scores for divers, students' scores are based on agreed-upon standards for what students should know and be able to do. Teachers, parents, and members of the community develop the standards, based on actual student work, in a public process. They state clearly the qualities demonstrated by the top levels of performance. That way, like divers, the students know what the judges are looking for, and they can learn to assess their own performance and improve. And teachers can work with them to bring them up to the highest levels. As Grant Wiggins asserts, the goal of the new measures is "standards without standardization."

The new assessments thus represent a new way of knowing what students know. We will know if a student knows math, for example, if she can demonstrate that she can confront a situation that requires mathematical reasoning, gather data, apply the appropriate mathematical principles, and communicate her results. That is a far cry from knowing that she is in the seventy-fifth percentile on a math test that asked her to choose the correct answers to problems handed to her. And if teachers teach in ways that enable students to do well on the new assessments, they will be fostering learning.

These ideas make intuitive sense to anyone who has ever taken a conventional test, whether in school, to earn a driver's license, or for any other purpose. Even when we do well on a test, we often feel that our responses do not truly reflect what we know or are able to do. In many cases, we recognize that we have gotten a high score as a consequence of some lucky guessing. At other times, we do poorly even though we feel we know the subject, because the questions do not allow us to show what we know.

Many educators recognize this as well and believe that the changes the cognitive scientists are urging reflect good teaching. Some leading reformers have tried to push schools in the same direction. One of the leaders in the reform movement is Theodore R. Sizer, a professor of education at Brown University. Sizer is the head of the Coalition of Essential Schools, a network of about 300 high schools dedicated to redesigning themselves to promote student learning. According to Sizer, "The purpose of education is not in keeping school but in pushing out into the world young citizens who are soaked in habits of thoughtfulness and reflectiveness, joy and commitment."

For Sizer and his colleagues, the way to create such a school is to start by defining those habits—what students should know and be able to do when they graduate. These definitions become the school's standards, just as the math teachers' council created standards for math education. They reflect the content and skills that are worth knowing, not just the number of hours a student must sit in classrooms. Then, working backward, teachers and administrators can create an education program that enables students to reach the standards. Thus the key element in redesigning a school is creating new forms of assessment that allow students to demonstrate their skills and knowledge, based on standards for performance. Sizer calls these assessments "exhibitions," and he sounds just like the cognitive scientists in arguing for them:

> Why an *Exhibition?* The word clearly states its purpose: the student must Exhibit the products of his learning. If he does that well, he can convince himself that he can use his knowledge and he can so convince others. It is the academic equivalent of being able to sink free throws in basketball. . . . To shoot baskets well one needs to practice. To think well one needs to practice. Going to school is practicing to use one's mind well. One does not exercise one's mind in a vacuum; one rarely learns to "think" well with nothing but

tricky brainteasers or questions embedded in a context that is neither realistic nor memorable. . . .

The final Exhibition is a "test," yes; but it is really an affirma-
tion for the student herself and for her larger community that what
she has long practiced in school, what skills and habits she has
developed, have paid off.[26]

Over the past few years, a growing number of schools, such as
the Littleton schools and O'Farrell, have worked with these ideas,
attempting to set standards and put in place new forms of assessment that seek to capture the qualities Sizer writes about. At the
same time, designers of some external assessment systems, particularly at the state level, have also taken such lessons to heart and
have created new systems aimed at measuring in new ways the
knowledge and abilities reformers consider essential.

In many respects, these state-level efforts are particularly significant. Because of the strong influence of external tests on school
practices, these new assessments hold the potential for transforming instruction in large numbers of classrooms. In addition, they
expand the conversation about school reform, since the assessments
serve as the basis for public discussion about the goals and quality
of schools. Moreover, the new systems also pose an enormous challenge, one that the pioneering states are only beginning to address.
Because they are intended to affect classroom practice, the assessments in many cases have some sort of high stakes attached to
them—that is, there are consequences attached to the results. But
assessments used for high-stakes purposes face different requirements
than those used solely within the classroom. They must provide
information that is sound and credible; otherwise, policy makers,
parents, and teachers could draw erroneous conclusions about student performance. And those wrong conclusions could cause harm:
a young person could be denied a high school diploma on the basis
of a mistaken judgment.

The new assessments also raise questions about the capacity of schools to enable students to reach the standards they are striving for. As we have seen in Littleton and San Diego, the new assessments demand substantial changes in curriculum and instruction. But as difficult as those changes are for a single school, they are many times more difficult for a state, where most teachers are accustomed to teaching in traditional ways. As a result, when states implement new assessments and compare student results to new standards for performance, the initial results appear low. This fact, together with a fear that high-stakes assessments could be used to punish students or schools that have not had the opportunity to learn what the assessments expect, has prompted a call for standards for *schools* as well as for students. This proposal has been one of the most hotly debated aspects of the shift toward standards and new assessments.

We will examine the obstacles the designers of the new systems face, as well as some findings about the quality of the new types of assessments. But first let us look closely at some of the pioneering state-level efforts to develop new standards for student performance and related systems of assessments. Then we will look at the most dramatic aspect of the shift in thinking about student performance: the idea of national standards and national assessments.

Chapter Four

Pioneers in the State Houses

Like many state education officials in the 1980s, Richard P. Mills, Vermont's commissioner of education, felt the pressure to hold schools accountable for student performance. As in other states, business leaders and legislators in Vermont were by 1988 beginning to clamor for information on student and school achievement to determine if the money spent on education was paying off in student learning. Unlike most states, however, Vermont had no statewide testing program to provide that information.

The absence of a state test was typical for Vermont, a state where many key policy decisions are made by citizens gathered in town meetings, not by lawmakers in Montpelier. But as the demand for information grew, Mills decided to meet it rather than have it imposed on him and the state's schools. And he wanted to do it in a way that would respect the state's town meeting tradition.

At the same time, Mills also wanted to apply the most current ideas in education reform. Though new in his post as Vermont's chief school officer, Mills was a longtime veteran of the national education scene. Prior to arriving in the Green Mountain State, he had served as the education adviser to Governor Thomas H. Kean of New Jersey, one of the leading "education governors." During his tenure, Kean had won a reputation as an innovator—and battled some powerful groups in the process—with such proposals as creating alternative routes to teacher certification and sponsoring the nation's first "academic bankruptcy" law (authorizing the state to take over failing school districts).

Given his own and his state's background, Mills, prodded along by the state's teachers, came up with an unusual answer to the accountability question—one that put Vermont in the forefront of the shift to new forms of measuring student performance. His answer was not only to test students statewide in two subjects—mathematics and writing—and in two grades—eventually state officials agreed on fourth and eighth grades—but to test them in a variety of ways, providing what he called a "balanced portfolio" of information on student performance.

First, the state would administer a fairly traditional test, possibly linked with the National Assessment of Educational Progress, that would indicate how Vermont students performed compared with each other and with students from other states. The other parts of this "balanced portfolio" were completely new, however. In addition to the uniform test, Mills proposed assessing students' performance on the basis of portfolios of work they completed in each of the two subjects throughout the year. And as a third component, he suggested evaluating what students considered their best piece of work, culled from the portfolios. "Teachers don't want to reduce the richness of a year's work to a single score," Mills said.[1]

Of course, using alternatives to traditional tests to evaluate student performance is not completely new. As we have seen, schools are developing new methods of assessment that tap a broader range of student abilities and spur transformations in teaching. What *is* new is the use of such methods to let policy makers and the general public know what young people know. As a report by the congressional Office of Technology Assessment (OTA) states, "Whatever the specific tasks involved, this move toward testing based on direct observation of performance has been described as 'nothing short of a revolution' in assessment. Given that performance assessment has been used by businesses and military training for many years, and by teachers in their classrooms as one mechanism to assess student progress, the real revolution is in using performance assessment as part of large-scale testing programs in elementary and secondary schools."[2]

In that revolution, Rick Mills and the latter-day "Green Mountain Boys" in Vermont are leaders at the barricades. But they have plenty of allies. According to the OTA, thirty-six states assess writing using direct writing samples and twenty-one states have implemented other types of performance-based assessments. Most of these, however, are in pilot or experimental form, the report points out. But more and more states are enlisting. In one project, led by the Council of Chief State School Officers, states are teaming up to develop new assessments jointly. Twelve states joined forces to create a new science assessment, for example, while another six states created one in history.

School districts, too, are shifting to new measures of student performance. A handful of districts, such as Pittsburgh and San Diego, have led the way, and many others are quickly following suit. About a dozen large city districts, for example, have teamed up with the American Federation of Teachers and Boston College to form the Urban District Assessment Consortium to share ideas and test new assessments. The consortium's first performance-based assessments were tried out in Boston in the 1992–93 school year.

As we will see, the largest effort to develop a new assessment system incorporating performance-based assessments and portfolios is a privately funded project led by the National Center on Education and the Economy and the Learning Research and Development Center at the University of Pittsburgh. Known as the New Standards Project, the effort involves nineteen states and six school districts.

Though these various efforts differ from one another, they generally share many of the characteristics mentioned previously that distinguish the new ways of measuring student performance. Students demonstrate what they know and are able to do by constructing their own responses to questions or, in many cases, formulating their own questions. The tasks are often based on real-world problems. Students may be able to demonstrate their abilities in a variety of forms, including writing, speaking, or video. And they are judged according to agreed-upon standards for what they should know and be able to do.

Like the teachers at Mark Twain Elementary School, Littleton High School, and O'Farrell Community School, educators in states and school districts that have implemented the new assessments say they have improved instruction by encouraging teachers to focus on the kinds of activities curriculum reformers and cognitive scientists say will help enhance student learning. And by setting standards for student performance, teachers and students as well are getting a clearer idea than they ever had before of what high-quality student work looks like.

But using such assessments as measures of accountability poses unique problems as well. If consequences are going to be attached to the results, the assessments must be technically sound. They must provide information that parents and members of the public want in ways that the constituents think are valid and understandable. As we will see, educators and researchers have not yet solved all of the problems presented by the new assessments, and states and school districts are therefore moving cautiously. But educators and researchers are tackling these problems, because they are convinced that changing the way of knowing what young people know is essential if all students are to attain high levels of learning.

Vermont: "Looking Beyond 'the Answer'"

For fourth- and eighth-graders in Vermont, the age-old student question—"Will this be on the test?"—is ancient history. Unlike their peers around the country, Vermont students get to decide for themselves what is on the "test."

In fact, the portfolio system was designed not to look like a test at all but to be virtually indistinguishable from regular classroom instruction. Instead of evaluating student abilities by taking students out of classrooms, asking them questions, and determining whether they answered right or wrong, the portfolio program is aimed at examining the quality of the work students perform during the course of a school year. By doing so, the program gauges a broad range of abilities, not just whether students can recall facts or solve relatively simple problems quickly. As a state department of education publication puts it, the portfolios are aimed at "looking beyond 'the answer.'"[3]

In addition, and perhaps most important, the system offers parents, policy makers, and the general public a chance to see what students know and are able to do, not just how they performed in comparison with other students. The results are released not just as scores published in the newspaper but as actual portfolios displayed in "school report days," which are similar to the town meetings for which the state is famous. The portfolios open up a window on school practice and student performance that in most states is closed. Commissioner Mills says that when he visits schools, he has an easy way of finding out how students are doing: he reaches for the milk cartons that hold their portfolios, takes them out, and reads them. That tells him a lot more than numerical scores. Thus while the portfolios are designed to provide accountability, the state program in practice serves many purposes.

Under the program, which was created by teams of teachers from throughout the state, fourth- and eighth-grade students compile portfolios of classroom work in writing and mathematics. The writing portfolios are designed to assess a range of types of writing. Although the contents can vary, the writing portfolios must include the following: a poem, story, play, or narrative; a personal response to a cultural event, current issue, math problem, or scientific phenomenon; a "best piece," chosen by the student; and a letter that explains the best piece and why it was chosen. In addition, the portfolio must also include writing from subject areas other than English/language arts. (For fourth-graders, the portfolio must include one such piece; for eighth-graders, three such pieces.)

The portfolios are evaluated by students' own teachers; however, a sample of portfolios and best pieces are then rescored by another group of teachers at the regional level. If the scores differ, the scoring is "moderated" by a leader from the regional network. The scoring measures the work according to five criteria: purpose, or the degree to which the piece establishes and maintains a clear purpose; organization, or the degree to which it illustrates unity and coherence; details, or the extent to which details are appropriate to the writer's purpose and support the main points of the piece; voice and tone, or the degree to which the piece reflects personal investment and expression; and usage, mechanics, and grammar. For each criterion, teachers must indicate whether each piece in the portfolio, including the best piece, demonstrates those facets "extensively," "frequently," "sometimes," or "rarely." They then assign an overall rating to the portfolio for each dimension.

In math, students select five to seven pieces of classroom work for their portfolios. As in writing, the math portfolios are expected to include a range of problems, but unlike the writing program, there are few content requirements. Instead, the guidelines recommend that the portfolios include "applications" (or problems that demonstrate that students can apply knowledge they possess) and "investigations" (or explorations, data analysis, or research that leads to conclusions). The original guidelines also proposed including "puzzles" (or tasks dealing with logic and reasoning), but these proved too difficult to score. The pieces of the math portfolio are scored on a four-point scale according to seven criteria:

- Mathematical language
- Mathematical representation, or the use of graphs, tables, charts, models, diagrams, and equations
- Presentation, or the extent to which the piece is clear, organized, and detailed
- The student's understanding of the problem

- How the student solved the problem
- Why—decisions along the way, or the extent to which the student explained her reasoning
- So what?—outcomes of activities, or the degree to which the student solved the problem and generalized the solution

As these criteria suggest, the math portfolios are aimed at gauging students' abilities to solve complex problems and communicate their reasoning—the same abilities the National Council of Teachers of Mathematics is urging for all classrooms, but ones that are seldom tapped in most schools or on most tests. As an example of Vermont's approach, consider the following problem, along with a solution from an eighth-grader named Emily:

The Bantam family is going on vacation. The Bantams are planning to fly to Denver, Colorado, and then rent a car for eight days to drive through the Rocky Mountains to Yellowstone National Park and back to Denver. Mr. Bantam asked his daughter, Mary, to help him figure out the best deal on rental cars. They can choose from three rental car agencies, whose terms are shown below:

U-Can-Rent-It	Good Deal	Tri-Harder
Daily Rates	Daily Rates	Daily Rates
Mid-size	Mid-size	Mid-size
$38 per day	$42 per day	$48 per day
75 miles free per day	100 miles free per day	Free unlimited mileage
$0.32 per mile over 75	$0.30 per mile over 100	$2 per day for 4-door
Full tank gas	Full tank gas	$12 one time fuel chg.
		1/2 tank gas

In addition, Mr. Bantam belongs to a travel club that gives him 10 percent off the total bill if he rents from "Good Deal" and 5 percent off if he rents from "U-Can-Rent-It" but nothing off from "Tri-Harder." From which company should Mary tell him to rent the car?

There is a total of 1126 miles to go from Denver to Yellowstone and back again. I found this out because in our atlas there is a mileage guide. It has Denver on it and Yellowstone Park. The distance between it is 563 miles. Then for turning around, I multiplied it by 2. Days total—8 days

U-Can	Good	Tri
$38	$42	$48
x 8 days	x 8 days	x 8 days
$304 for 8 days	$366 for 8 days	$384 for 8 days

1126/8 = 140.75 traveled each day, rounded miles days to 141

U-Can	Good	Tri
141 − 75 = 66	141 − 100 = 41	unlimited
miles/free	miles/free	
66 to pay for	41 to pay for	
66	41	
x .32/mile over 75	x .30 mile over 100	
21.12	12.3	

U-Can	Good	Tri
$304 trip	$336 trip	$374 trip
+ $21 mileage	+ $12 mileage	————
$325 trip	$348 trip	$384 trip
Full gas	Full gas	1/2 gas
+ 0	+ 0	+ 12
$325	$348	$396

Tri is definently out—as it is the most and I haven't done the percent off and Tri doesn't have any off.

U-Can	Good	Tri
$325	$348	
x 5%	x 10%	
16.25	34.8	
$325	$348	
− $16	− $35	
$309	$313	$396

U-Can or Good are both fine. It is only a matter of $4. You could pick either—you might prefer one closer, of if you really want to—you could save $4.

This weekly challenge was really easy. People had been talking about how hard it was and how long it took but it only took me 45 min. After I found the # of miles (very easily) I thought I was stuck. But I decided to start with finding how much each car cost for eight days. From there I just went on and on. Only I did not know what $12 one time fuel chg. meant until I asked my dad.

When I showed this to my mother she said "I just did that." It turned out she was trying to find the best car rental for our trip during vacation.

Tri-Harder was a real rip-off. I didn't even try what it would cost with a 4 door. It would of been more, obviously. $400 for 8 days/ Plus the $10 fuel chg. and only 1/2 tank of gas.

It really doesn't matter which of the 2 other car deals Mary chooses. Its just a matter of $4. I would choose then what one was closer and what car I liked better and what one had better gas mileage etc.

According to the scoring guide developed by Vermont teachers, on this problem Emily earned a level 3 for understanding the problem, how she solved the problem, and decisions along the way;

she received a 1 for the "So what?" category, since she simply solved the problem and stopped; she received a 4 for her presentation, which was well organized and detailed; and she received a 1 for both mathematical language and mathematical representation, which were lacking.

Clearly, we know a lot about what Emily knows by seeing her response to a problem like this, judged according to the standards developed by Vermont teachers. We know that she can collect data, consider evidence, and present solutions to a real-world problem (a problem so real that Emily's mother had solved a similar problem herself). And we know from cognitive science that if teachers employ such exercises as part of their daily instruction, students like Emily learn.

Eager to implement such a program in their classrooms, teachers in Vermont responded enthusiastically to the portfolio assessment system. Although the state had asked only forty-eight school districts to take part in a pilot assessment in the 1990–91 school year, another ninety asked to participate as well. When the state moved to full implementation a year later, however, not all districts were ready. Several, including Burlington, the state's largest, elected not to send their math portfolios to be scored. Burlington officials explained that they had not had sufficient time to reform their math instruction. But educators there and throughout the state clamored for professional development, forming seventeen regional networks for training that would help them revamp their instruction.

The networks, moreover, were closely tied to the portfolios. Using actual examples of student work—such as the example above—teachers discussed the work in relation to the scoring guide. The idea behind these networks was to give teachers a strong sense of the standards for student performance and of high-quality work. Then the teachers could go back to their home classrooms and share their understanding with their students, thus helping them to bring their work up to the highest standards for performance.

Did the portfolio assessment lead to changes in instruction? A study by the RAND Corporation, conducted for the National Center for Research on Evaluation, Standards, and Student Testing, suggests that it did. Through surveys of math teachers and interviews with a representative sample of principals, the researchers found that the state's educators considered the portfolios a burden—but a worthwhile one. Both principals and teachers agreed that the program took a considerable amount of time to implement. On average, the study found, teachers spent six hours a week on the portfolios: two to three hours preparing for portfolios, two to three hours in classroom activities related to the portfolios, and one hour scoring and evaluating portfolios. In addition, nearly all teachers said they took part in some form of state-sponsored training to implement the program. One teacher, according to Daniel M. Koretz, the director of the study, gave up a job as a church organist because of the burdens involved in the program. Students, the teachers estimated, spent about fourteen hours a month on portfolios, including seven hours doing portfolio-related tasks, four hours revising, and three hours organizing the portfolios.

Notwithstanding those burdens, teachers and principals said the program changed instruction for the better. Sixty percent of the principals agreed that the program had had beneficial effects on math instruction, and only three principals said that the effects were negative. Among the positive effects the principals cited were an increased emphasis on problem solving, a decreased emphasis on textbooks and drill and practice, and greater attention to communication in math—precisely the areas the assessment was intended to tap. Teachers also said they were placing more emphasis on teaching problem-solving and communication skills. For example, two-thirds of the fourth-grade teachers and three-fourths of the eighth-grade teachers said they were spending more time on written reports of math-related projects since implementation of the portfolios.

In a sign that the portfolios also served as better ways of knowing what students know, the vast majority of teachers also said they
had changed their opinion of students' math performance as a result
of their portfolio work. As one teacher put it, "Many portfolio
entries indicate students' thinking processes and their learning
process or the lack of such." Significantly, three-fourths of the
fourth-grade teachers said that low-ability students were "occa-
sionally" or "often or always" more successful on portfolio tasks,
although many also said such students found the tasks difficult.
However, some teachers in the pilot year said the emphasis on written work in the portfolios may have provided a misleading impression of student abilities. "A few students are quite good in
mathematics and think logically but cannot express themselves in
writing as well," one teacher said. "Simply reading their pieces may
not give a true picture of their math skills."

Nevertheless, the overall impression was positive. Perhaps the
most significant vote of confidence in the program came from principals. About half the principals surveyed said they had expanded
portfolios beyond the grades involved in the statewide program, and
another 10 percent said they planned to do so. In 9 percent of the
schools, portfolios were used by every teacher. "This suggests that
the program is seen as a successful and worthwhile educational
intervention by practitioners, despite the fact that most of our
respondent principals also perceived the program as burdensome,"
the RAND researchers stated.[4]

Armed with such knowledge about the program, Vermont officials began to expand it. Sixty teachers from seventeen high
schools piloted the use of math portfolios at that level, and additional schools were expected to follow in the 1993–94 school year.
In addition, teachers and state officials are now discussing the
development of portfolios for the arts and for community service
programs.

But as effective as portfolios are as instructional tools, they also
must serve as measures of student performance. And on that score,
as we will see, the RAND researchers found a different story. Exam-

ining the first year's implementation, the researchers found serious problems with the scoring of the assessment, and they recommended changes accordingly. But state officials remain strongly committed to the program.

California: Following Frameworks

Although Vermont's efforts have attracted the attention of educators nationwide, they have not spawned legions of imitators. Some see Vermont as too small and too idiosyncratic to serve as a model for other states. What works in a state with only 7,000 teachers who live a short drive from one another (and in which town meetings are the rule) may not work in a large state—one in which hundreds of thousands of teachers live hundreds of miles apart and often cede decisions to representatives in school districts or state capitals.

An experiment across the country from Vermont may show whether alternative assessments can work in a large environment. The nation's largest state, California, has embarked on an ambitious effort to create a new way of assessing what its five million students know and can do. The effort has hit rocky shoals. If it ultimately succeeds, it could demonstrate that new forms of assessment can work anywhere.

California has for several years sought alternatives to traditional measures of student performance. In 1987, it introduced to the California Assessment Program (the statewide testing program known as CAP) a writing assessment that asked students to compose essays, not simply answer questions about writing. The following year, it added open-ended questions to its twelfth-grade mathematics test to give students an opportunity to generate their own responses to questions. The state department of education also held a conference in 1989, entitled "Beyond the Bubble," to explore alternatives to fill-in-the-bubble assessments and to consider ways to implement them.

To educators in the state, particularly then–state superintendent of public instruction, Bill Honig, these forays into new assessment were essential pieces of the school-reform puzzle. Honig came into office in 1983 convinced that schools had to change and that the way to start changing them was to define what should be taught and learned and then build the rest of the system around those goals. Toward that end, with Honig's leadership, California created "curriculum frameworks" in key subject areas that outlined a program for instruction from kindergarten through grade twelve. In many ways, these frameworks departed substantially from practice common to most classrooms—and most tests. The math framework called for a greater focus on solving problems using mathematical reasoning rather than arithmetic computation. The English/language arts framework called for integrating reading and writing so that students write about, and thus develop deeper comprehension of, what they read. And it urged that all pupils read real literature, not the bowdlerized stories some textbooks use.

Honig knew, though—and if he had not known, teachers would have told him—that teachers would never implement the ideas in the frameworks as long as the assessments did not match them. But his plans to revamp the assessment program along the lines of the frameworks came to an abrupt halt in 1990, when the program got caught in the crossfire between Honig and Governor George Deukmejian. In the midst of a heated feud over the education budget, Deukmejian eliminated all funding for CAP—a small amount in dollars but a high priority for the superintendent. Rather than curse the darkness, though, Honig lit a candle: he appointed a statewide task force to recommend a completely revamped assessment program. Their proposal became the basis of legislation signed into law in 1991 by the new governor, Pete Wilson, which restarted the program Honig four years earlier had tried to begin, with a new direction and a new name: the California Learning Assessment System, or CLAS.

The new system represents a substantial shift from the earlier program and is one of the most ambitious efforts yet undertaken in creating a new way to assess student performance. Under the law, every student in grades four, eight, and ten will be tested in reading, writing, and mathematics, and every student in grades five, eight, and ten will be tested in science and social studies. In the past, the state has tested a sample of students at various grades and provided scores that showed school performance. But Governor Wilson, who wanted parents to have information about their children's progress, insisted on providing scores for individual students, a demand that considerably broadened the scope of the program— there are about a half million students in each grade—as well as raising the stakes.

In addition to the massive scale, the new program also differs from the old CAP in its substantial reliance on new forms of assessment. The math assessment consists of a combination of multiple-choice questions and performance tasks and takes an entire class period. The reading and writing assessments take a total of three class periods, usually spread out over three days: on the first, students read a complete short story and answer a series of open-ended questions; on the second, they work in groups to discuss aspects of the story and how it relates to their own lives; on the third, they write an essay, based on their own experiences, related to a theme of the story.

In addition to the assessment tasks, which students are to complete "on demand," the state also plans to develop a portfolio assessment that would measure student performance on a range of work completed during the school year. State officials had originally planned to add a third component as well, one that would measure student performance on "curriculum embedded" tasks. Under this plan, schools would ask all students to complete a long-term project as part of their regular classroom work. But when some teachers objected that the proposed assessment would take too much time out of regular instruction and would amount to a state-mandated curriculum, that component was dropped.

To create the new system, California officials chose an unusual solution. The state department of education contracted with four of the major commercial test publishers—CTB Macmillan/ McGraw-Hill, the publisher of the California Achievement Test and the California Test of Basic Skills; Riverside Publishing Company, the publisher of the Iowa Test of Basic Skills; the Psychological Corporation, the publisher of the Metropolitan Achievement Test; and the Educational Testing Service, the administrator of the Scholastic Aptitude Test—to help develop and operate the program. The department sought out the firms because the task of building the system was far beyond the capabilities of a small state government office. The companies, with vast experience in building tests, could lend their expertise to help California do it right. But the companies' involvement also showed that a shift to a new method of measuring student performance need not represent a clash of right versus wrong. Although the commercial publishers continue to earn their bread and butter from traditional tests, they recognize that many states and school districts are looking to performance assessments as well. As company officials have said, both types of measures provide important information about student performance, and both together provide a fuller picture of student abilities.

CLAS aims at tapping a broader range of student abilities than traditional tests and at providing information on what students know and are able to do, not just how they compare with one another. The math assessment, for example, attempts to see how students solve math problems and communicate their understanding, not simply how many right answers they have. Likewise, the reading assessment is designed to enable students to demonstrate their understanding of a text, reflecting what cognitive scientists say readers do when they understand written material. According to a document prepared by the California Department of Education,

Reading . . . is the process of constructing meaning through transactions with text. In this view of reading, the individual reader assumes the responsibility for producing an interpretation of the text, guided not only by the language of the text but also by the associations, cultural experiences, and knowledge that the reader brings to the interpretive task. Rather than believing that meaning resides solely within the words on the page, this view of reading emphasizes the role of the individual reader in making meaning through a process that brings together textual and contextual evidence and the distinctive experience and perspective of the reader as meaning-maker.[5]

To gauge reading ability in that way, the assessment offers students a variety of ways to construct their meaning. Students' knowledge and skills are evaluated on the basis of their responses taken as a whole. The text itself provides space in the margins to permit students to record their thoughts and questions as they read. The assessment then asks students, in a question that is completely open-ended, to indicate their initial responses to the story. Using words or graphics, students can discuss their opinions and ideas about the story, any connections they may draw to their own lives, or any other response. The assessment then includes from four to seven additional questions that allow students to provide further evidence of their understanding. Some of these refer to specific passages in the text; some allow students to use graphics or drawings to indicate what a character in the story may have been thinking or feeling. The final question provides students with a last opportunity to "tell anything else" about the text.

As we can see, this assessment offers quite a different way of gauging children's abilities. Instead of giving students a short passage and asking them a set of questions to test their initial memory or comprehension, the CLAS assessment provides students several chances to show what they understand. There are no simple right or wrong answers; instead, the assessments are scored on a 1-to-6 scale according to standards for performance developed by a team of teachers. Student performances rated 6 ("exemplary" performances) are insightful, discerning, and perceptive; they show connections with and among texts; they take risks by entertaining challenging ideas; and they challenge the text by questioning the writer and agreeing with or disagreeing with the text.

By contrast, those rated 4 ("thoughtful" reading performances) construct thoughtful and plausible interpretations of the text, but they rarely take risks and only sometimes challenge the writer. Those rated 3 provide literal but superficial interpretations of the whole work, while those rated 2 indicate that students do not grasp the whole. Those rated 1 show minimal understanding.

Here is an example of an eighth-grader's response, rated a 6, to an essay by Banesh Hoffman about Albert Einstein. The example is presented exactly as written during test conditions, so it includes misspellings and syntactical errors:

1. *What is your first response to the story? Take a few minutes to write your ideas, questions, or opinions about this story.*

Originally, I thought of Einstein as a prestigious and notable person that thought of basically impossible, but true, theories. After having read this, I discovered that Einstein was much more than a scientist and mathematician. He was a person who educated himself with music and the art of nature. Einstein didn't care that something worked, he cared how and why something worked and what place it held within the universe. Einstein's life was much like the life of anyone else. He was directly effected in what happened in the world or with his own life. All Einstein really cared about was living life. He didn't seem like the person who did the things he did just to receive fame and fortune. To my generation, Einstein would never seem a simplictic man, his theories and numbers are all too original and confusing. However, he was a simple man, he lived life by fulfilling the necessities of food and shelter and by conversing with the world and nature.

2. *Think about Einstein as a person and a scientist. In the split "profile" and below it, use symbols, images, drawings, and/or words to give your ideas about Einstein the person and Einstein the scientist.*

Einstein the person	Einstein the scientist
deep in thought	religious
friendly	theory of relativity
musician	controversial
wife	gravitational theory
saddened	knowledge came to him
wondered about the world	$E = mc^2$
Christmas w/those carolers	revolutionized physics
late to speak	prodigy in thinking
not infant prodigy	

3. *Explain how the symbols, images, drawings, and/or words in your "profiles" represent your ideas about Einstein.*

As a person: Einstein was a friendly man who was effected by the things that happened to him. He was easily saddened after they used his theory to build an atomic bomb and by his wife dying. Einstein probably did more thinking as a regular person instead of some infant prodigy that had a lot of knowledge. He wondered about the world in order to achieve so much knowledge. Even though he was late to speak, he indulged himself by putting together puzzle pieces of nature.

As a scientist: Even though Einstein had no formal religion, he received his knowledge from religion. His religious-scientific ideals about thinking got him to come up with the theory of relativity, gravitational theory, and $E = mc^2$. Einstein's scientific ideals that got him to become so controversial was because of simplicity. His simplicity in thinking and reasoning made him a prodigy, a mix of knowledge and common sense.

4. *Think about Einstein the scientist and Einstein the person. Choose an example from the reading selection that shows how Einstein's personal characteristics affected him as a scientist.*

Einstein's personal characteristics affected him as a scientist. One example of this was when Einstein signed the letter from the scientists who were afraid the Nazis were building an atomic bomb. Because of this, U.S. also decided to build an atomic bomb, a total disregard for the value and respect of life. After this incident, Einstein always had a look of sadness and remorse in his eyes even though he took no part in it. Einstein's scientific theory was the key in building the bomb. However, as much as any other scientist would praise himself for being so brilliant, Einstein punished himself by feeling responsible for those who died. Einstein's personal beliefs had a strong effect on how he applied his scientific concepts. Einstein had too much respect and appreciation for the balance of nature, the world, and life in order to be responsible for the atomic bomb.

5. *Based on your reading, if you were to talk to Einstein, what would you want to say to him or ask him?*

If I were to talk to Einstein, I would ask if all the things he did in his life were worth it. Of course Einstein made a giant leap for society, but would he rather live a more normal life instead of having to pay for his fame? Another question that I'd ask him is what he held in his life most dear to him. And if it was his wife, I'd ask if he would give up all of his theories just to have her back. I'd also ask him why his simplicity within his theories and nature was so important.

6. *How did this reading selection change, add to, or reinforce your ideas about scientists in general, or about Albert Einstein specifically?*

I think that reading this selection greatly reinforced my ideas about Albert Einstein specifically. What I already knew about Einstein had already been proved to be true in the story. However, I also learned how Einstein was able to become such a genius. It was mainly his beliefs about beauty and the world and how simplicity is the root to all complicated things. I never thought this to be true before the story, I had always believed Einstein was incredible because he was of sheer brilliance and smarts.

7. *This is your page to tell anything else you want about your understanding of this reading selection—what it means to you, what it reminds you of, how it relates to your own life, or whatever else you think is important about the reading selection.*

After having read this selection, I think I've reinforced my views on life. I've realized that a person can be successful without having to give up your connection to the world. I learned about how Einstein was a finely tuned instrument that harmonized with the world to make beautiful music. Einstein has become a symbol of the dedication that has committed his whole life in the areas of science. As much as I wish I could be like Einstein, I also feel sympathy for him and the sadness that he felt when his ideas were abused. I have also found a new way of thinking and believing through reading this story. I've realized that a person has got to keep things simple and has got to work with the balance of time and of the universe in order to accomplish things. But basically, I've learned that working with the essentials of life is the most important goal.

Imagine a classroom where that kind of reading takes place! It is a classroom where students read rich literature that offers them the chance to explore well-drawn characters and compelling stories. It is a classroom where students and the teacher engage in thoughtful discussion to draw out the meaning of what they read. And it is a classroom where students write a lot, to enable them to communicate their understanding, as the eighth-grader in the above example did so well.

In writing, as in reading and math, the California assessment seeks to allow students to demonstrate their abilities and judges them according to standards for high-quality writing. Students actually receive two scores: one for rhetorical effectiveness and one for the use of writing conventions such as spelling and grammar.

The state has also piloted assessments in history/social science and science and plans to add those to the battery. Like the reading and math assessments, the history and science assessments include a mix of questions that ask students to use what they know and communicate their reasoning. The history/social science assessment, for example, contains multiple-choice questions; justified response questions, which ask students to select an answer and justify their choice with historical evidence; short-answer questions, which are several paragraphs in length and may be based on primary-source documents; essay questions, which take about thirty minutes to write and also may be based on primary-source documents; and historical investigations, for which students work in groups and write their responses individually, based on an analysis of primary- and secondary-source materials.

As an example of the type of performance California educators rate as exceptional, consider the following essay by a tenth-grade student, printed here exactly as written under test conditions:

Essay Topic: Some argue that the Treaty of Versailles laid the basis for World War II. Do you agree or disagree? Explain your position using historical evidence.

The twentieth century started with the devastating world war which killed millions of people and expanged many cities both in Europe and Asia. The World War finally ended in 1918 with the victory of the Allies. The leaders of the victor countries, Clemenceau from France, Lloyd George from England, Orlando from Italy and President Wilson from the United States gathered in Paris to discuss peace terms. Of all the resulting treaties, the most important was the treaty of Versailles which dealt with the fate of Germany. Although this treaty terminated World War I, dissatisfaction remained among many countries and its severe punishments against the loser countries or the Axis Power, caused serious problems resulting in increase in antagonism among countries. German leaders would call for revenge and fascist governments would overthrow the pre-existing ones in Italy, Germany, and Spain. In the turmoil following the treaty of Versailles, these problems grew and led to the second World War which turned out to be even more devastating than any previous wars.

The treaty of Versailles was a meeting among the Big Four: Orlando, Clemenceau, Lloyd George and President Wilson. Although these leaders did not aim to do so, the peace settlement in Paris resulted ultimately in the Second World War. The leaders demanded high indemnities from Austria, Germany, and Hungary and took away lands giving them away to other countreis. Areas inhabited by Germans, including the Sudentainland were taken from the Germany Empire and were sceded to the Polish corridor, Yugoslavia, and France taking Alsace-Lorraine regions were understandable, but taking German-inhabited areas were unforgivable the German people. The nationalism among the people especially of the German people grew stronger as a result of this treaty. In addition, the German people surrendered because they thought that the basic points of Wilson's Fourteen Points would be followed. When the principle of "peace without glory" was rejected, Germans viewed this as a "stab in the back" and got very angry. All war guilt was blamed on Germany in the famous Article 231, and the Punishments were severe. The forming of the league of Nations was achieved, but without the participation of major countries such as the United States, it was doomed to failure. The severe punishments not only strengthened antagonism, but also caused economic dislocation. It was impossible for larger coutries to pay high indemnities when their industry had been destroyed by the war. Unemployment rates went up and inflation raised prices of food and daily goods by million and billion times. Depression and social problems soon spread throughout Europe and unstabilized political conditions in many areas. Fascist dictators took over in Germany by Hitler, Italy by Mussolini and in Spain by Franco. These dictators will justify their aggression by nationalism and will cause struggles among countries.

The Treaty of Versailles marked the successful victory of the Allies, but it also started the problems which could bring about the Second World War. Even Orlando was dissatisfied for not gaining the ports of Filne. How dissatisfied were the Germans and the Austrians? Severe punishments brought also the economic depression in the 1920's leading to the rise of dictatorships in various areas. Weather or not the leaders of the treaty of Versailles could have avoided World War II is a question that will be discussed for centuries.

Like Vermont, California is relying on classroom teachers to score the assessments for state purposes, but because of the sheer size of the state, the effort poses a daunting challenge. During the summer of 1993, the first year the program was implemented, some 2,500 teachers gathered at thirty-seven sites across the state for four-day scoring sessions. After a day of training, in which teachers learned the performance standards, they read hundreds of student papers and gave them scores. Highly trained teachers, known as "table leaders," read behind the teachers on a sample of papers; if the scores differed on any given paper, the table leader's score would prevail.

As large as that effort was, it represented only a fraction of the training and scoring that will eventually be needed, since the state provided only school-level results in the program's first year. Eventually, to provide individual student scores, many thousands of teachers will have to be involved. The state's goal is to train a cadre of teachers who can go back to their home schools and train their colleagues to conduct the scoring there. But this must be done carefully; the scorers must be well trained so that the scores can be reported reliably. And even now, the scoring is very expensive. The state must either pay teachers for their additional time or—if teachers are released from the classroom for scoring—it must pay for substitute teachers to take over the teachers' classrooms while they are away scoring assessments.

But as in Vermont, officials in California insist that teacher involvement is essential if the assessment is to do anything to improve instruction in the state. Evaluating the assessments gives teachers an understanding of the kind of tasks they should be using in their classrooms. Teachers see that, rather than give students endless lists of three-digit multiplication problems, they should provide opportunities for them to use their knowledge to solve problems and communicate their understanding, as the assessment does. Scoring also helps teachers see what high-quality student work looks like. Instead of evaluating papers by comparing Jimmy's work to Maria's, teachers can compare each student's work to the standards. And since the standards were derived from actual student papers, teachers know that a 4 in math and a 6 in reading can be achieved. In fact, they say their goal is to bring all their students up to that level. That way, every child can indeed be above average!

But if the initial results of the program are any indication, California has a long way to go to achieve that goal. Although many teachers hailed the CLAS program as a welcome improvement over the old state test, and one that conformed to the instructional goals of the curriculum frameworks, large numbers of teachers had not, by the time of the first assessment in 1993, transformed their classroom practices to reflect the frameworks' recommendations. As a result, many students had not yet had the kind of instruction CLAS was measuring, and the first-year results were generally low. Very few students attained the top levels of performance; most hovered around a score of 2. These results set off alarms throughout the state, particularly in schools that had generally performed well on state tests. Although the average performance in these schools (in the first year, the state reported only school-level results) exceeded that of traditionally low-performing schools, few students in any school reached the highest standards.

In time, student performance may rise; and indeed, many teachers expect the new assessment to spur changes in instruction. As long as the public was judging schools on the basis of test scores, these teachers reason, the tests, not the frameworks, guided instructional decisions. But now that the test matches the curriculum frameworks, teachers have an incentive to implement the proposals called for in those documents.

Whether they will get the opportunity to do so, however, is an open question, since, as in Littleton, controversy threatens to scuttle the system. Like the Colorado school board candidates, critics in California have objected to the types of knowledge and skills the new assessment attempts to tap and the ways it attempts to measure student abilities. The critics have attacked on several fronts.

First, they raised objections to a reading selection used in the assessment, an excerpt from the short story "Roselily" by the Pulitzer Prize–winning author Alice Walker. After a newspaper published a passage from the story in an article about the assessment, a group of parents and conservative Christians complained to the state board of education, charging that the story was antireligion (the passage in question was a monologue by a young Christian woman who was about to marry a Muslim man). In response to the complaint, the board pulled the story from the test. Although state department of education officials explained that their move was necessary because identification of the story compromised test security (since those who knew that the story would be on the test could read it in advance and gain an unfair advantage over those who did not), board members admitted that the political controversy also played a role in their decision. Board members also voted to remove two other stories from the list of materials that could be used on the test, although they later rescinded that decision in the face of strong objections from teachers and civil liberties groups.

In addition to challenging the reading passages, critics of CLAS also objected to the test itself. Using arguments that echo criticisms of new standards for student performance in other states, the critics contended that CLAS measures students' attitudes and beliefs, not their academic knowledge and skills. They claimed that having students bring their own experience to bear in their written responses to reading passages—which, as the state department of education has explained, is the way students demonstrate their understanding—is a way of judging and keeping track of students' family lives. In an extraordinary move, two students won a court order allowing them to exempt themselves from the test; following the ruling, the state department of education allowed local districts to allow parents to opt out of the test as well. Then, in a major blow, Governor Wilson put a halt to the program by vetoing a legislative attempt to revamp it. Acting shortly before the 1994 election, in which he sought a second term, Wilson said the proposed revision would not provide individual scores soon enough, and placed too much emphasis on performance assessments.

The objections in California, like those in Littleton, reflect a fundamental difference over the direction education should take. Like the parents who took over the school board in Littleton, the critics of the California Learning Assessment System envision an education system much like the one they themselves went through rather than a new approach that values students' abilities to use knowledge to solve problems and communicate their reasoning. Unlike the reformers in Colorado, though, the reformers in California have had a long history of building support for their vision, both as they pushed for introduction of the curriculum frameworks and as they argued for adoption of the new test. They have vowed to try to restore the program in 1995.

Kentucky: The Second Revolution

To paraphrase an old saying, some states reform their own education systems, and some have reform thrust upon them. Kentucky had reform thrust upon it by a cataclysmic event: the state supreme court threw out the entire state education system and ordered the legislature to build a new one from the ground up.

The court's 1990 ruling came in a case, similar to others filed in many states, that challenged disparities in funding for education. As in New Jersey, Texas, Montana, and other states, the Kentucky court agreed that wide gaps in spending on schools within the state violated the constitutional guarantee of educational opportunity for children from poor communities. But the court went farther than judges in other states and concluded that, because of the funding disparities, the education system itself was unconstitutional.

The ruling presented officials in the Bluegrass State with an opportunity as well as a challenge. They did not have to graft reforms onto something that was already in place, as did their counterparts from other states; they would be starting fresh. They could benefit from the experience and expertise of reformers from around the country. And the court ordered a massive increase in funding for education to alleviate the disparities.

Acting immediately to meet the court's deadline, the legislature quickly passed the Kentucky Education Reform Act of 1990 (KERA), the most comprehensive education reform package ever adopted by a state. The law did everything from mandate family resource centers for poor families to ban nepotism by school boards. But the focus of the entire law was student performance, and its centerpiece was a new way of measuring that performance. The law spelled out six goals for student learning and established a strict accountability system to ensure that schools would enable students to meet the goals. Under the law, schools where students improve their performance are eligible for cash bonuses; schools that do poorly face possible sanctions, including having their teachers placed on probation or dismissed. To Thomas C. Boysen, the state's first appointed commissioner of education, who was hired to implement the law, KERA represented the "second-greatest revolution in American education." In the late nineteenth and early twentieth centuries, he said, schools opened their doors to provide access to education for every child. KERA, he added, "has the intention of giving every child the right to succeed in school."[6]

In keeping with the law's focus on student performance, educators in the state first spelled out seventy-five "valued outcomes," or statements of what students ought to know and be able to do, and created a new assessment system to measure performance on the outcomes. Administered to every student in grades four, eight, and twelve, the Kentucky Instructional Results Information System shares many of the elements of the new assessment methods that we have already looked at. It asks students to use what they know to solve real-world problems. It allows them to demonstrate what they know and are able to do, not just find the right answer. And it evaluates students not by comparing them to one another but by weighing their work against agreed-upon standards for performance.

Like Vermont's system, the Kentucky assessment consists of three parts: a multiple-choice and short-answer component, linked to the National Assessment of Educational Progress; a set of performance tasks; and a portfolio of students' best classroom work collected throughout the school year. The results are rated according to four performance levels: novice, apprentice, proficient, and distinguished. But because the reform law holds schools accountable for student performance, the state provides only school-level results, not scores for individual students.

However, contrary to Vermont, the assessments are scored by a private firm, Advanced Systems in Measurement, not by teachers (although portfolios are scored by teachers). That way, state officials maintain, the results will have credibility with a public that might be skeptical of teachers' judgments.

Such credibility is essential, for Kentucky officials have insisted that the scorers be tough. They want to get across the point that their standards are high; they were designed for schools to aim for, not to reach on the first try. (The slogan for KERA is: "In Kentucky, we just expect more!") The officials also launched a public relations campaign to explain the standards, presenting the results on satellite television, administering assessment tasks to school board members, and undertaking other efforts. This campaign made the standards for student performance well known and a topic of public debate; to that extent, it was successful, since a comprehensive understanding of the standards is necessary to the new method of measuring student performance. Still, the results came as a shock in the state, particularly in schools where students had been accustomed to high scores on standardized tests. Overall, only 10 percent of students in the first assessment performed at the proficient level, and a tiny fraction reached the distinguished level.

But as state officials were quick to point out, the assessment measures abilities that traditional tests seldom tap and demands the kind of performance that few schools emphasize. But Kentucky's goal was to encourage schools to change. A state department of education document reads, "Kentuckians eager for positive results in education reform may find first-year assessment scores lower than they would like. Remember: the assessment program is new to Kentucky teachers and students. It requires teachers to make significant changes in the way they teach; it asks Kentucky students to meet new standards and use information in new ways. Student and school scores gradually will show improvement."[7]

As an example of the Kentucky standards, consider the following, from an eighth-grade science assessment:

> *A few years ago, scientists collected seeds from a particular type of tomato plant. Half of the seeds were kept on earth while the other half were sent to outer space in a shuttle and remained in space for a long period of time. When the seeds came back to earth, anyone interested was given some of the "earth seeds" and some of the "space seeds" for experimentation.*
>
> *Suppose you were given some of each type of seed.*
>
> * *List all of the variables you could control in designing an investigation using the seeds.*
>
> * *If all of the variables you listed could be controlled, what hypotheses or research questions could the investigation test?*
>
> * *What kinds of data would need to be collected to test these hypotheses?*

Here are examples of student responses at each level, exactly as written:

Level 4

Variables: Soil, sunlight, fertilizer, water temperature, and altitude.

Whether or not the space seeds could still seek out sunlight, if altitude affected them, if differt fertilizers harm one, but not the other, if the space seeds can withstand varying temperatures.

heighth, weight of soil, amount of daily water, fertil., and sunlight, and visible effects

Level 3

First of all, in order to see which grows better you need soil, water, the seeds, sunlight, and a container. Make sure the materials are the same for each. Over a period of time keep a chart of how quickly they grow and how healthy they are. If you need any answers to questions concerning the growth, check the table.

Level 2

1. wa\:r amounts, sunlight amounts and the amount of nutrients are the control variables.

2. My hypothesis would be that the space seeds grow faster because of the exotic atmosphere they were in.

3. Data collected would be finding out where and what atmosphere they were in.

Level 1

amt. of sunlight

amt. of water

As this example indicates, the Kentucky assessment system asks students to do more than simply recall facts about scientific procedures and concepts; it asks them to demonstrate their understanding of science by using their knowledge to construct solutions to problems that could occur in the real world. The problem is complex—or, as cognitive researchers say, "ill-structured"; there is no neat solution that is either right or wrong. The students are judged on the quality of their responses, or the extent to which they show that they know scientific principles and can articulate them.

In time, Kentucky officials hope that this kind of exercise will become an integral part of instruction. Toward that end, they encourage teachers to administer and score assessments in grades other than four, eight, and twelve, when the state assessments are given. Using a football metaphor appropriate to this sports-crazy state, Kentucky officials refer to the local assessments as "scrimmages" designed to help students and teachers prepare for the "varsity" level.

Eventually, Kentucky officials hope, the standards for student performance will become second nature to teachers and students. As Commissioner Boysen put it, students should approach learning the way divers approach the ten-meter board. "A ninth grader trying out for the diving team can formulate quickly in his mind what a 9.9 dive is," he said. "We want him to figure out what it will take to put together a number 4 portfolio."[8]

Is it working? Early returns suggest that the changes are happening slowly and unevenly, but that they are indeed happening. In releasing the results of the 1993 assessment after the second year of the program, Boysen noted that performance improved at the fourth- and eighth-grade levels but declined at the twelfth-grade level compared to the previous year. But he noted that some schools that had revamped their curricula and instruction had showed dramatic gains, and he predicted that other schools will read the message from the results and show similar improvement. Reaching again for a sports metaphor, Boysen observed, "This is half time. Just as football teams use the intermission to make adjustments necessary to win the game, schools must analyze their first-half performance and make adjustments."[9]

As critics were quick to point out, though, the state needed to make adjustments too; and in 1994, the legislature adopted what Boysen called "mid-course corrections" to the reform act. Responding to complaints that the twelfth-graders did not take the test seriously (since they did not receive individual scores and thus knew that their performance would have no bearing on their future), the legislature agreed to move the high school test down to the eleventh grade, when students' "senioritis" hasn't yet set in. In addition, lawmakers agreed to postpone for a year the date when the state would reward or punish schools for improving or declining performance. Schools had charged that they would not have sufficient time under the original schedule to make the changes needed to boost performance. But despite lingering opposition to the entire system, state officials remain committed to it.

Like districts in Littleton and San Diego, the states of Vermont, California, and Kentucky are at the forefront of efforts to find a new way of knowing what young people know. But they are not the only ones. Maryland, for example, launched a performance-based assessment system in 1991. That program, operated by CTB Macmillan/McGraw-Hill, the publisher of two major standardized achievement tests, measures the abilities of students in grades three, five, and eight in a range of subjects. But unlike the other programs we have seen, Maryland's school performance assessment program has an unusual twist: the tasks are deliberately designed to cross subject-area boundaries. For example, an eighth-grade task used in 1992 asks students to listen to statements and read a number of documents about the buffalo in U.S. history. Students are then asked to respond to the materials, to show that they can read and understand maps, and to respond to written passages, among other tasks. Taken together, the parts of this exercise tap knowledge and skills in social studies, reading, writing, and language usage. Similar cross-disciplinary tasks measure science and mathematics abilities taken together, as well as science taken individually; reading; writing abilities; and other skill groupings.

Other states, too, have implemented new ways of measuring student performance, and many more are laying plans to do so. Moreover, the number of states setting standards and creating new assessments is likely to grow in the wake of President Clinton's 1994 school reform legislation, the Goals 2000: Educate America Act, which authorizes federal grants to states that design standards-based reform plans.

But as the examples in this chapter indicate, the shift to new standards and assessment systems is still evolving. The states described in this chapter, which have moved perhaps the farthest, are still working out the problems inherent in such dramatic changes in the way they do business. And they have not completely turned their back on the old system; all the states still maintain some form of traditional testing, whether in their new programs or in existing standardized tests. Other states, meanwhile, are still experimenting with new forms of assessment. The task of creating new methods of measuring student performance is fraught with difficulties, both political and technical. We will examine the issues involved and look at what some researchers are discovering will work. But first let us examine a movement that has paralleled the efforts of schools and states to find a new way of gauging student performance: the growing interest in some form of *national* standards for student performance and a *national* assessment system.

Chapter Five

A Test for the Nation?

Midway through the first year of his term, George Bush, who had pledged during the 1988 campaign to be the "education president," summoned the governors of the fifty states to Charlottesville, Virginia, for an extraordinary meeting to discuss education policy.

The 1989 "education summit" was rich with symbolism. For one thing, it was only the third such gathering of chief executives in history. President Theodore Roosevelt had held the first, on the environment, and President Franklin D. Roosevelt had convened a similar meeting on the economy. Because of this symbolism, education was instantly elevated to the top of the national agenda.

The meeting's setting was also evocative. The meeting took place on the campus of the University of Virginia, an institution founded by the first education president, Thomas Jefferson. And by gathering participants outside of Washington and involving the governors, the organizers signaled that education was a national concern, not just a federal one.

What emerged from the summit was also extraordinary. For the first time in the nation's history, the chief executives pledged to set national goals for education and to hold themselves accountable for attaining them. The goals, moreover, were ambitious; some called them unrealistic. Announced in early 1990, they stated that, by 2000, every child will enter school ready to learn; the high school graduation rate will increase to at least 90 percent; all students will demonstrate competence in challenging subject matter; U.S. students will be first in the world in mathematics and science achievement; all adults will be literate; and all schools will be safe and drug-free.[1]

While cynics pointed out that the elected officials would be long out of office by the target year, the goals themselves reshaped the agenda in education policy. Although in the past, education was almost solely the province of local school boards and state governments, the national goals placed the federal government and national organizations at the center of the action. And by focusing on student performance, the goals lent urgency to the call for a new way of knowing what young people know. Just as educators in schools such as Mark Twain Elementary and in states such as Vermont were defining what students ought to know and be able to do and developing new assessments to allow them to demonstrate that students have attained the standards, officials responding to the goals began to call for national standards for student performance and a related national system of assessments. "We're not going to figure out whether the national goals are met," said Albert Shanker, the president of the American Federation of Teachers, "unless there is some form of national assessment."[2]

Does the United States not already have national standards and tests? One could argue that, in some sense, we do. The vast majority of classrooms rely on textbooks as the primary mode of instruction, and the variety of textbooks on the market are more alike than different. Similarly, the widely used standardized tests—those that, as we have seen, influence teachers' practice—tend to measure the same things, although there may be slight variations in emphasis.

These standards, though, are implied, not explicit. They are not the result of a systematic effort to determine what all students should know and be able to do. Rather, they are the result of 15,000 separate decisions by 15,000 school boards in 15,000 school districts. Moreover, despite the overall pattern of uniformity, different standards exist for different groups of students. Those young people bound for selective colleges, who tend to be concentrated in relatively affluent areas, are likely to receive challenging instruction in demanding coursework. But those students represent a small minority of the student population in this country. For the rest—particularly the 40 percent of students not going on to higher education—instruction tends to be shaped by textbooks and tests. And these students are disproportionately from minority groups and low-income families. Their standards are a far cry from what the goals demanded: that all students demonstrate competency in challenging subject matter.

One prominent indicator of the low overall standards for student achievement is this country's recent performance on international mathematics and science tests. While the best performers in the United States have held their own with their peers from other nations, the average U.S. performance has been near the bottom in international rankings. One significant exception to this pattern has been in reading, however. In a thirty-two-nation test of reading literacy in 1992, U.S. nine-year-olds outperformed those from every nation except Finland, and U.S. fourteen-year-olds did nearly as well.[3]

In addition to lacking common standards, the United States at the time of the Charlottesville summit had no national test. The idea of a national student test was not completely new, but it had never gotten off the ground. Admiral Hyman Rickover, the nuclear scientist, had proposed such a test as far back as the 1960s, after studying European education systems and concluding that tests set high standards for student performance in those countries.[4] Rickover helped persuade his former protégé, Jimmy Carter, to study the issue when he became president. Congress in 1988 even authorized the creation of a national test, but that provision was never implemented. The idea met a wall of criticism from educators, who argued that a national test would fly in the face of this country's strong tradition of local control over education, which held that local school boards, not the federal government, should decide what should be taught. Educators also warned that a national test could narrow the curriculum and could harm disadvantaged youths.

The federal government does, however, operate one well-respected national barometer of student achievement: the National Assessment of Educational Progress. Sometimes known as the "nation's report card," as noted earlier, NAEP periodically tests elementary, middle school, and high school students nationwide in reading, writing, mathematics, science, and other subjects. Its reports are considered the best available indications of trends in student achievement in those subjects over time. As we have seen, NAEP has provided credible evidence that student performance, particularly in math, increased during the 1980s.

The assessment has also documented, as we have seen, that the growth in achievement has largely been at the level of basic skills, not in more advanced competencies. By including questions that tap a range of abilities, NAEP has shown in a dramatic way the types of questions students can answer. It also asks students for background information on their families and coursework to enable researchers to determine which students tend to answer which kinds of questions correctly.

Despite its high regard among educators and policy makers, though, NAEP has two major limitations. One is its traditional view of measuring performance. For the most part, NAEP has generally consisted of paper-and-pencil tests that ask students multiple-choice questions outside of their regular classroom work. The scores are based only on whether students answer questions correctly or not and on how they perform in comparison with their peers. In recent years, however, NAEP has begun to incorporate new techniques that go beyond the traditional methods. A number of tests have added open-ended questions that ask students to generate their own answers, in writing or by using figures. The writing assessment asks students to write essays and evaluates them on their overall skill. And in 1990, NAEP conducted a special study to evaluate students' classroom writing, a possible first step toward including in the assessment a portfolio of student work.

A second limitation of the national assessment, at least according to those seeking a way to measure student progress toward the national goals for education, is the fact that it is a *survey*, not an individual student test. In fact, the way NAEP is constructed, there is no "NAEP test." Rather, the students who participate take a short test that includes several questions from an overall battery of several hundred. That way, NAEP can show achievement on a broad range of knowledge and skills without asking students to sit for hours. But because of this methodology, NAEP can provide information only on the nation as a whole and for four large regions— the Northeast, the Southeast, the central states, and the West. As we have seen, Congress expanded NAEP in 1988 to allow state-level comparisons; and in 1991, the project provided information on eighth-graders' mathematics achievement for thirty-seven states as well as for the nation as a whole. But even while it approved the expansion, Congress limited it to a trial basis and prohibited the results from being used to provide comparisons of school districts, schools, or individual students. The congressional action was motivated, in large part, by the same concerns that had held off consideration of national testing.

A Changed Equation

Despite educators' deep-seated suspicion of a national test, Albert Shanker and others in the late 1980s contended that the national goals had changed the equation. In order to find out if students could truly "demonstrate competence in challenging subject matter," we would need a new way of knowing what young people know, they argued: national standards that would define what all students should know and be able to do and new assessments that would gauge individual student performance against those standards.

Some supporters believed that the new assessments could do on a national level what the new assessments states and schools were implementing promised to do at those levels: improve student performance and instruction as well as provide a better way of measuring students' abilities. Shanker, in particular, promoted the idea that a testing program with real consequences for students would provide an incentive for all students to work hard in school. Now, he argued, students do little work, because they know they can get away with it. They can get into most colleges and jobs without showing what they know and are able to do, because admissions officers and employers seldom look at more than a diploma (which simply shows that a student showed up in high school for four years). If students knew that they could get into college or a job only by demonstrating their abilities on an examination, he argued, they would work hard to do well on the test.

Others argued that a national assessment that truly tapped students' abilities to solve problems and think, like the ones being tried out at the local and state levels, could steer instruction toward those abilities. We have seen that teaching to the standardized tests in place in most schools has fostered rote drill in basic skills. If a test were in place that measured high-level reasoning, teaching to that test would be beneficial.

Public officials, echoing Admiral Rickover, pointed to the experience of other countries in arguing for national tests. The low ranking of U.S. students on cross-national tests of mathematics and science suggested to some that standards in this country were too low. By contrast, in European nations and Japan—which generally outperform the United States on such tests (and, these advocates pointed out, increasingly in the global marketplace)—national tests set high standards for students. In an effort to dramatize the standards set in other countries, Lynne V. Cheney, chair of the National Endowment for the Humanities, published a book in 1991 that included questions from examinations in the humanities from France, Germany, England, Japan, and the European Community. Her book, *National Tests: What Other Countries Expect Their Students to Know*, drove home the point that those nations ask a lot of their students. As Cheney wrote in the introduction, "Could American students answer the questions that the French ask about the foreign policy of the United States? That the British ask about

American progressivism? That the European schools ask about South Carolina's secession? Do we expect our students to know American history as well as other countries expect their students to know it? Do we expect our students to know the history of other nations in anything approaching the detail with which they are expected to know ours?"[5]

Of course, Cheney's answer was no. But in some respects, the questions were loaded. As she conceded, the exams included in her book did not represent the expectations for *all* students. In many cases, only a fraction of college-bound secondary students took and passed the exams. For instance, two of the examples in her book were history selections from German exams known as the *Abitur,* which are used for college entry. But as Cheney pointed out, only 23.7 percent of "the relevant age group" in that country in 1986 qualified for university entrance. Still, the exams indicate that standards in the United States could be higher than they now are and that tests are a way of setting standards and measuring progress toward their attainment.

Another element that changed the equation in the discussion of national testing was the emerging consensus among educators nationwide on what should be taught. With mathematics teachers leading the way, educators from a number of subject-matter organizations began in the mid 1980s to redefine what to teach—and how to measure what students have learned. These efforts, most of which won wide praise for their vision, buttressed the call for a new national system of assessments to replace the existing array of tests, which no longer matched the curriculum goals.

The earliest and best-known of the curriculum reform documents was *Curriculum and Evaluation Standards for School Mathematics,* issued by the National Council of Teachers of Mathematics (NCTM). That report, released in 1989 and widely hailed by the math education community, outlined a program for instruction from kindergarten through twelfth grade that represented a substantial shift from most existing practice. In place of schools' emphasis on computational drill, the NCTM called for a substantial use of calculators and computers to enable students at all ages to use mathematical reasoning to solve problems. It likewise called for assessments that measure problem-solving abilities, not just the ability to do calculations. In addition, the council recommended developing students' abilities to communicate in mathematics, something that traditional tests do not measure.[6]

In addition to the math teachers, other national organizations were also forging an agreement on what to teach. The American Association for the Advancement of Science, the world's largest scientific group, launched an ambitious effort to redesign science instruction in elementary and secondary schools by first defining what students ought to know and be able to do in the field. In a 1989 book, *Science for All Americans*, the association's Project 2061 outlined what young people should leave high school knowing and understanding about science, and it urged less emphasis on memorizing lists of science facts and more emphasis on developing scientific "habits of mind."[7] At the same time, the National Science Teachers Association undertook a national reform project to restructure junior high and high school science instruction to deepen students' understanding of biology, chemistry, and physics.

Other subjects proved more contentious, but educators nevertheless attempted to define what should be taught in English, history, civics, and geography as well. In English, a coalition of organizations representing teachers from kindergarten through graduate school urged greater emphasis on enabling youngsters to become readers, writers, and thinkers and less emphasis on factual knowledge about works of literature. This view came under sharp attack from such figures as William J. Bennett, former secretary of education, and E. D. Hirsch, Jr., a University of Virginia professor and the author of *Cultural Literacy*, who argued forcefully for a core set of information that all students must know. To underscore his point, Hirsch included in his book a list of names, places, and titles

that he felt all literate Americans should know, and he later published a series of books outlining core content for children at all
grade levels—from first grade on up.[8]

Educators in social studies, meanwhile, were divided: those who
argued for placing the chronological study of history at the center
of the field opposed those who contended that history should be
taught in the context of geography, political science, economics,
and other social sciences. The field was also riven by an intense
debate over the appropriate balance between the study of Western
civilization and that of other cultures. Secretary Bennett, among
others, maintained that schools should emphasize the West as the
wellspring of this country's common culture. But others argued for
a more multicultural approach that would reflect the background
of the increasingly diverse student body.

Not all educators endorsed the idea of redefining what should
be taught in key subjects, however. To some educators, notably
Ernest L. Boyer, the former U.S. commissioner of education, the
curriculum reform efforts only served to reinforce traditional subject-matter boundaries at a time when schools should shatter those
boundaries. Especially as instruction connects schooling to the real
world, Boyer and others argued, teaching should not be compart-
mentalized into disciplinary blocks.

Nevertheless, the national debate on the content of instruction
helped move along the discussion on national standards and assessments. Another event that spurred that discussion was the hotly
controversial attempt by the National Assessment Governing
Board, the policy-setting arm of the National Assessment of Educational Progress, to set national standards for student performance—to state how well students *should* perform. Beginning with
mathematics, the board attempted to define what students ought
to know and be able to do, in order to determine "how good is good
enough" on NAEP tests. Using these new standards, the board now
reports the number of students who perform at the "basic," "profi-

cient," and "advanced" levels on the assessment rather than providing just a simple numerical score. But as we will see in the next chapter, their efforts have come under sharp attack.

The emergence of the national goals, the national curriculum standards, and the national performance standards thus set the stage for a renewed debate over a national assessment. But there was another new element as well: support from the American public. According to the 1989 Gallup Poll on education, 69 percent of the public favored a national curriculum and 77 percent backed national testing programs.[9]

The Tide Toward Testing

Convinced that the time was ripe for a national system, Shanker presented his argument for such a test to fellow members of President Bush's Education Policy Advisory Committee, a panel of twenty-four prominent educators, public officials, and business leaders, including the chief executive officers of Xerox, IBM, the University of Tennessee, and Cornell University. The panel, which met periodically to give advice to Bush's domestic-policy staff, began to consider the testing idea seriously in the fall of 1990. Paul H. O'Neill, the chief executive officer of the Aluminum Company of America and the chairman of the advisory panel, argued that a national test would provide information that the existing array of tests failed to provide. "My own view," O'Neill said, "is that we need a test that can be given to individual children, the results of which can be given to the child and teacher to better inform all parties how the child is gaining the competencies necessary to be a participating citizen." Although O'Neill argued that the test should be voluntary, he noted that, if it were of high enough quality, most schools would elect to use it.[10]

The chorus in favor of some form of national testing began to grow. The Secretary's Commission on Achieving Necessary Skills (SCANS), a U.S. Labor Department panel studying the changing workforce and the abilities young people need to succeed, considered new assessments to measure the skills of entry-level workers. The National Education Goals Panel, a group of governors and Bush Administration officials brought together to measure progress toward the national education goals, weighed a new assessment system to gauge student achievement. Saul Cooperman, the former commissioner of education in New Jersey, called for a federally funded mandatory test for all twelfth-graders. The College Board, the sponsor of the Scholastic Aptitude Test and the Advanced Placement examinations, launched plans to create syllabi and examinations for "capstone" high school courses.

President Bush, meanwhile, placed the issue into the political arena by calling for national testing as part of his America 2000 school reform plan, which was released after he had received a report from his advisory panel. Although the testing proposal became somewhat overshadowed by a heated debate over school "choice," the plan sent to Congress recommended "world-class" standards in five core subjects—English, mathematics, science, history, and geography—and a set of voluntary "American Achievement Tests" tied to the standards. The plan proposed that the tests would be used to "foster good teaching and learning" as well as to gauge student performance against the standards, and it urged colleges and businesses to use the tests in admissions and hiring decisions. In announcing the plan in April 1991, Bush said he would like the first test, for fourth-graders, to be ready by the fall of 1993. The week after his plan was announced, Bush met with math educators and challenged them to come up with assessments that matched their standards for instruction.[11]

Perhaps the most forceful advocate for national standards and assessments was Governor Roy Romer of Colorado, the first chairman of the National Education Goals Panel. Romer, a Democrat, was a surprise choice to lead the panel; the Democrat who had spearheaded the goals effort was Bill Clinton. But amid criticism from Congress and elsewhere that the goals process was overly political, the governors selected one of their own who had an election behind him—Romer was reelected in 1990 and would not face the voters again until 1994—rather than one about to enter the presidential contest.

But anyone who thought the choice of a little-known western governor would take the spotlight off the goals did not know Roy Romer. A lawyer from a tiny sheep-farming town in eastern Colorado, Romer used his skills as a quick study and a blunt speaker to turn the national goals into topic number one in education circles. For much of 1991 and 1992, Romer was everywhere: any time more than a dozen educators gathered, it seemed, Roy Romer was there, often with a well-thumbed copy of the math standards, to talk about the need for standards and a new way of measuring student performance.

Romer usually made his case in his typical, straightforward style, appealing to political reality as well as common sense. As a governor, Romer knew that states were moving rapidly to create their own standards and new assessments, as we have seen. What was needed, Romer would say, was a national framework to give shape and guidance to the state efforts. He also offered familiar analogies to explain what he called "standards-based education." Sometimes he would compare the gauge of education performance that he was after to a CAT scan. When you go to a doctor, he would say, the doctor will tell you where you are physically, what health is, and what to do to move toward health. An assessment system would tell you where your education performance is, while the standards would correspond to health.

More frequently, Romer would draw on his experience as a pilot to explain standards and assessments. No one wants to fly with a merely above-average pilot, he would say; students, like pilots, must all attain *high* standards for performance. And assessments tied to the standards cannot be abstract paper-and-pencil tests. To find out if a pilot can land a plane, Romer would say, a flight instructor does not ask multiple-choice questions. Rather, the instructor takes the prospective pilot up in a plane, shuts the engine off, and says, "Land it." Though some educators were dubious about his analogies— learning trigonometry is not the same as learning to fly an airplane—Romer kept the issue of national standards and assessments high on the education agenda.

Amid all the discussion, one plan began moving toward implementation. The National Center on Education and the Economy, a research and policy group based in Rochester, New York, and the Learning Research and Development Center at the University of Pittsburgh teamed up to form the New Standards Project to test the development of a national examination system. Fueled by more than $2 million in private foundation grants, the group enlisted seventeen states and six school districts to begin trying out the system.

The New Standards Project stemmed from a 1990 report by the National Center on Education and the Economy that called for dramatic reforms to improve the skills of the American workforce. Among its proposals, the report, entitled *America's Choice: High Skills or Low Wages?*, called for ambitious standards for student performance and new assessments to measure performance against the standards. If at about age sixteen students could demonstrate that they had attained the standards, they would earn a "certificate of initial mastery" that would entitle them to employment or further education or training.[12]

The New Standards Project also bore the stamp of Lauren Resnick, the director of the Pittsburgh center and, as we have seen, one of the leading researchers in cognitive science and education. Resnick was also a member of the Labor Department's SCANS commission and an adviser to the goals panel. Citing research that she and others had conducted on how children learn and how current tests impede learning, Resnick argued for a completely new assessment system that would enhance student learning. "We can't continue with the kinds of tests that are driving the American system," she argued. "The goals today for schools are not the goals of 40 or 50 years ago, yet we have the tools of 40 or 50 years ago."[13]

According to Resnick, the new assessment system should be national in scope so that it encourages high levels of learning for all students, not just those bound for selective colleges. It should be an examination *system* to allow flexibility for school districts and states to develop assessments tied to national standards, as well as something to study for to provide an incentive for students to work hard in school. And it should reflect a new way of knowing what young people know: in place of traditional tests that consist of abstract questions handed to students outside of the regular class-room setting, the new system should include performance assess-ments, projects, and portfolios that provide students opportunities to demonstrate what they know and are able to do, judged against standards for high performance.

To create the new system, the New Standards Project gathered together teachers from several of the participating states to deter-mine whether it was possible to set common standards for student performance. To find out, officials asked the teachers to grade stu-dent papers from another state: California teachers graded Texas students' writing, Texas teachers graded Vermont's, and so on. To their surprise and delight, the project's leaders found a high degree of agreement among teachers across states on what constitutes high-quality student writing. Next, teachers from all of the participating states met to develop sample assessment tasks in English/language arts and mathematics. The idea turned test-making on its head. Instead of first determining the content and skills educators wanted students to know and be able to do and then developing tasks to measure those, the New Standards effort asked teachers to create tasks they wanted students to complete and then, from those, to determine what it was they wanted students to know and be able to do.

The teachers then tried out their tasks in their classrooms, and after some refinement, they and project officials whittled down their products into a handful of tasks that were administered in a pilot test to some 20,000 fourth-graders in May 1992. The following year, a second pilot was administered to some 50,000 fourth- and eighth-graders. In 1994, the project administered a full-scale mathematics exam to a sample of students in each of the states and school districts that composed the group.

The following problem, administered to eighth-graders in 1992, illustrates the New Standards approach:

Suppose you work for a shoelace company. You receive the following assignment from your boss.

Assignment

We have decided to sell laces for sports shoes. We will sell different lengths for shoes with different numbers of eyelets. We will offer sports shoes that have 4 eyelets all the way up to 18 eyelets (no odd numbers, of course). No one has ever sold so many different lengths for sports shoes before. You have to figure out what lengths to make and which lengths go with which shoes, based on the number of eyelets.

We collected some data from store customers last week. It is confusing because there haven't been many lengths available. That means that sometimes the customers have had to use lengths that are too short or too long. That's not what we want! We want a unique length for each number of eyelets.

Data from Store Customers with Sports Shoes

Customer I.D.	Lace Length (inches)	Eyelets (numbers)
A	45	8
B	54	10
C	26	4
D	63	14
E	63	12

Data from Store Customers with Sports Shoes, continued

Customer I.D.	Lace Length (inches)	Eyelets (numbers)
F	36	8
G	54	12
H	24	4
I	72	14
J	54	12
K	72	16
L	72	18

Write your decisions about lace length so the advertising people making the sign can understand it. They want a table, so customers can look up the number of eyelets and find out the length of lace. They also want a rule, so customers who don't like tables can use the rule to figure out the lengths. Don't worry about making it pretty, they will do that, just make sure the mathematics is right. You better explain how your decisions make sense, so the advertising people will understand.

Thanks! Your Boss, Angela

Write a response to your boss Angela's assignment:

• A table that shows for each number of eyelets (even numbers only) how long you have decided the laces should be

• A rule that a customer can use to figure out the length based on the number of eyelets. Don't forget the bow. If you can, express your rule as a formula.

• An explanation of your decisions (tell why they make sense)

The student responses were scored by teachers who met for a week in Utah. They rated the student papers on a scale of 0 to 4, with exemplary papers earning a score of 4+. According to the scoring guide, a 4 indicates that a student accomplished the task, preparing an accurate table and a general rule or formula that is clear and reasonable. A score of 3 indicates that the response gives evidence that the student can revise the work to a 4 with the help of a note such as "Please explain your formula." A score of 2 means that part of the task is accomplished, but there is a lack of evidence—or evidence of lack—in some areas. Responses earn a 1 if the task is misconceived, the approach is incoherent, or the response lacks any correct results. A 0 is reserved for no response or a response unrelated to the task.

As in Kentucky and other places that have tried new forms of assessment, the results of the New Standards assessment were poor. Only a third of the students earned scores of 3 or better on problems such as the shoelace problem, and only 10 percent attained the highest level. As other states and schools have discovered, these types of problems are new for many students—those who are accustomed to the relatively low-level skills demanded by conventional tests.

In the future, the New Standards Project is planning to broaden its scope by including an examination in science and a high school exam. The latter is expected to form the basis of the "certificate of initial mastery" proposed in *America's Choice*. In addition, New Standards is adding portfolios to its assessment repertoire. Like the "reference exams," the portfolios will be evaluated against common standards for performance. To help set the standards, teachers in the project are studying examinations and curricula from many countries with high-performing students and determining what the best of those countries expect from their youth. Their goal is to see to it that all students leave high schools in the United States with a level of knowledge and skills that is second to none in the world.

Meanwhile, as the New Standards Project was piloting its new assessment, the College Board had also moved toward developing its own version of a national testing system. Modeled after its widely acclaimed Advanced Placement program, the project, known as "Pacesetter," was designed to be a curriculum project as much as a testing project; it included a year-long syllabus and ongoing assessments as well as end-of-course exams. In the 1993–94 school year, the first Pacesetter course, a high school math course designed as a precalculus course, was piloted in fifteen schools in ten school districts. Grounded in the NCTM standards, the course differs sharply from traditional upper-level math courses, which are often highly abstract and theoretical. Pacesetter math is designed to enable students to use mathematics in real-world settings. Toward that end, it focuses on "case studies"—problem-solving tasks in which students demonstrate their understanding through the use of mathematical models or representations of the problems. The course relies heavily on technology, particularly graphing calculators, to depict such representations.

Like the New Standards Project, Pacesetter is aimed at setting high standards for all students and measuring their performance in new ways. The courses employ "embedded assessments," or assessments that students take throughout the course of the year to provide teachers with an ongoing record of progress. In addition, the College Board has developed end-of-course assessments—these include portfolios and performance events—designed to capture students' understanding of the entire year's work.

In addition to its math course and exams, the College Board is developing similar Pacesetter courses and exams in English and plans to develop them in science, Spanish, and world history as well.

Walls of Resistance

Like earlier proposals for national tests, the New Standards Project, Pacesetter, and the other calls for a national assessment system encountered stiff resistance. Many teachers, including those who strongly favored new methods of measuring student performance, feared that national plans could scuttle their own efforts to improve teaching and learning. Decisions about what students ought to know and how to measure that knowledge, they argued, should be left to local school communities—parents, teachers, and administrators—not to officials in Washington, D.C.

In addition, critics also warned that, despite the proponents' claims, national tests could end up measuring fairly low-level knowledge and skills, failing to set the promised high standards for performance. In making this argument, critics often cited the case of textbooks, which are generally aimed at a national audience. Because textbooks are expensive, and they must sell in California, Kansas, the Carolinas, and everywhere in between, textbook publishers cannot afford to go off on a limb and create books that risk alienating potential customers. As a result, publishers weigh each state's requirements and produce what former Secretary of Education William J. Bennett once called "bland porridge." Although some publishers have broken out of the pack and have produced high-quality books, the economics of the industry continues to dictate that they can publish only what the market will bear.

Some critics of the national test proposals also expressed concern that the new assessments could harm students and schools the way previous tests did, only more so. Many of the problems associated with tests that we have seen—narrowing the curriculum, accentuating the gaps between advantaged and disadvantaged students—have come about because high test stakes lead educators to focus on raising test scores, not raising achievement, particularly for low-scoring students. A national test, the critics pointed out, would only exacerbate these problems by creating even higher stakes. The critics also cautioned that, without any effort to upgrade school facilities and programs, the tests could erect a new, higher hurdle for low-income and minority students, who tend to fare less well than their more advantaged peers on tests. At particular risk, they claimed, would be children whose first language is not English; they would be at a severe disadvantage on an English-language test. If a national test were used to make decisions about students' placement and advancement in schools, disadvantaged young people could end up worse off than before. Firing a warning shot across the bow of the testing flotilla, the advocacy group FairTest organized coalitions of education and civil rights organizations to express concern about national tests. In one effort, a statement issued shortly after President Bush announced the national goals, some three dozen groups implored the president and the governors to resist using tests as a measure of progress toward education goals. The statement favored new methods of measuring student performance and expressed fears that a rush to hold children to new standards would force the nation to use conventional tests, with harmful consequences.

The critics' arguments resonated in Congress, which, despite passage of the 1988 measure authorizing a national test, had long been skeptical of the practice and was particularly concerned over equity. So when the Bush Administration and the nation's governors in June of 1991 created a panel to look into national standards and a related system of assessments, Congress, which had been left out of the Charlottesville meeting, sought to put brakes on the bandwagon. Following some discussion, Congress, the Administration, and the governors that month formed the National Council on Education Standards and Testing to examine the "desirability and feasibility" of national standards and assessments.

The thirty-two-member council, which quickly acquired the rather infelicitous acronym NCEST, was what one member called a typical Washington "Noah's Ark" panel: it consisted of two senators, two representatives, two governors—including Roy Romer— two state legislators, the presidents of the two teachers' unions, and a number of teachers, school administrators, testing and education policy experts, and government and business officials. Meeting monthly over a six-month period, the council heard testimony from educators and state officials on reforms in curriculum and assessment and formed task forces to consider standards, assessment, and the implementation of a national system. The council moved quickly, because the ground beneath it was shaking: during the time the council was in session, federal agencies awarded grants to the National Academy of Sciences and the University of California, Los Angeles, to develop national standards in science and history to go along with the math standards already established by the NCTM. And the U.S. Education Department also set in motion plans to award grants for standards-setting in other core subjects as well.

Unlike most blue-ribbon panels, which tend to hold their debates behind closed doors and show a unified front to the public, the standards council, in a reflection of the contentiousness of the issues it discussed, played out its disagreements in full view of its audience and the C-SPAN cameras. At one session, the congressional members balked at a proposal to endorse a national testing system beginning as early as 1993. At another, members heatedly debated a proposal to recommend a host of education reforms (such as full funding of Head Start) as part of a plan to ensure that all students are able to attain high standards for performance. At a third, several members objected to a suggestion that national tests be monitored to see whether they were used as intended. At yet another session, the council split evenly over a plan to set national standards for schools as well as for students.

In the end, the council agreed to issue a ringing call for a new way of knowing what young people know. Its final report, *Raising Standards for American Education*, released in January 1992, concluded that national standards and a related system of assessments were both desirable and feasible and proposed a new structure to oversee their development. Under this system, the National Education Goals Panel would form a National Education Standards and Assessment Council to certify as "world class" (as stipulated in Bush's America 2000 plan) the new standards and assessments, which would be developed by private and government agencies.

In its recommendation, the council suggested that standards consist of five components: an overarching "vision"; content standards, such as those developed by the National Council of Teachers of Mathematics, which define what schools should teach; student performance standards, such as those being developed by NAEP's governing board, which outline the levels of achievement students should attain; school delivery standards, which describe a school's capacity to enable students to attain the standards; and system performance standards, which indicate the extent to which school systems succeed in educating students to the standards. In a move that would prove hotly controversial, the council recommended that the school delivery standards should be set by the states themselves from among a set of standards developed by the states collectively. All other standards would be developed nationally.

Regarding assessments, the council explicitly rejected a single national test and instead proposed that "clusters" of states develop or acquire assessments that measure performance against the new standards. It also proposed a dual assessment system consisting of individual student tests and a national monitor of achievement, such as NAEP, and noted that it is "unlikely" that the same assessment instrument could accomplish all the purposes the system is expected to fulfill—purposes ranging from gauging performance against the standards to improving instruction to holding schools accountable for performance. The council also noted that "there is significant interest in the promise of performance-based assessments" but stopped short of recommending that all the new assessments be performance-based.[14]

Governor Romer, the council's cochairman (along with Governor Carroll A. Campbell, Jr., of South Carolina), called the council's report a "historic" step toward creating a new way of knowing what young people know. "This is the first time that there has been a national effort—from Congress, the Administration, the governors—intended to set standards for American education. It signals that we are serious about raising standards, and finding ways to do it that respect both local control and national leadership."[15]

Adding the Congressional Voice

But if Governor Romer thought the council's report heralded a national consensus on the issue, he was mistaken. If anything, the report served only to turn up the volume on the already noisy debate.

The newly intensified debate got under way before the ink was dry on the report. Even before the report was released, the Senate approved an amendment, sponsored by Senator Jeff Bingaman of New Mexico, a council member, that incorporated several of its recommendations, including creating the National Education Standards and Assessment Council. The amendment was attached to a bill that was drafted as a Democratic alternative to President Bush's America 2000 plan.

But on the day the NCEST report was released at a Washington news conference, a group of about fifty prominent educators and scholars—they insisted the timing was coincidental—issued a statement warning against a national test. The group cautioned that a national test could widen the gap between advantaged and disadvantaged students. They also asserted that a test would do little to change classroom practice and could stifle the reforms already under way in a host of schools around the country. "No one is talking about the fact that change is a local affair," said Ann Lieberman, a professor of education at Teachers College, Columbia University, and one of the organizers of the statement. "There is an assumption they can push people around like puppets on strings at the national level."[16] But in part because the council report proposed an assessment system, not a national test, as well as provisions to ensure that students have opportunities to meet the standards, several council members argued that the statement and the report were compatible. In fact, the statement's original list of signers included two members of the standards council.

Partly because of such words of caution, though, the House of Representatives declined to go along with the Senate and immediately approve the council's report. Instead, members of that chamber decided to hold a series of hearings on the issue. The hearings provided an opportunity for other critics to add their voices to the chorus urging caution.

Several of the critics who testified before the House panel warned that the NCEST proposal could create a powerful high-stakes assessment system that would place tremendous pressure on schools to focus on the assessments but would not necessarily boost achievement. Citing some of the research we have seen about existing testing systems, the critics noted that the proposed national system would share many of the same potentially harmful characteristics. "The research from the last ten years has shown us you don't have to go nearly that far [in placing consequences on test results] to get perverse effects on schools," testified Daniel Koretz of the RAND Corporation, who had found, in research discussed in Chapter Three, clear evidence that high test scores did not equal high achievement. "Teachers have gotten the message loud and clear that they would be rated on how kids score on tests. That's all it takes. The problem is, it simply hasn't worked in raising performance. I don't know why we would want to try it again when it hasn't worked before."[17]

In addition to challenging the effects of the system the NCEST report proposed, other critics also charged that the report left unanswered key questions that would determine whether the proposal for standards and an assessment system would be harmful or beneficial. In an influential report to Congress, the congressional Office of Technology Assessment (OTA) cited a dozen such questions, including these: Who will set the standards? What will happen to students who score low? What effects will national testing have on state and local efforts to develop new assessments that match local goals? Would all students be tested, or samples of students? "If a test or examination system is placed into service at the national level before these important questions are answered," the OTA report concluded, "it could easily become a barrier to many of the educational reforms that have been set into motion, and could become the next object of concern and frustration within the American school system."[18]

Other critics contended that standards and assessments alone would be unlikely to boost the level of student achievement, and they cited the experience of other countries as evidence. In a study conducted for the OTA, George F. Madaus of Boston College and Thomas Kellaghan of St. Patricks College in Dublin found that testing in other industrialized nations is quite different from the type proposed by the NCEST report and that factors such as teacher education and "inspectorates" (or independent observers who evaluate the quality of schools)—not just the existence of a testing system—explain the differences in student achievement between the United States and those nations.

Specifically, Madaus and Kellaghan found that the idea that only the United States lacks a national testing system is a myth. In Australia, Germany, Canada, and Switzerland, for example, provincial or state governments have substantial authority over the design and administration of tests. Moreover, Madaus and Kellaghan found that almost no country tests students before age sixteen, and most use tests to select students for scarce slots in higher education and training programs. Put another way, the researchers found that virtually no country uses tests for one of the primary reasons cited by the NCEST report: to monitor student or school progress toward national goals for student performance (and thus to spur schools to improve that performance). As the OTA stated in its report, "The rhetoric that advocates national testing using the European model tends to neglect differences in the history and cultures of European and Asian countries, the complexities of their respective testing systems, and the fact that their education and testing policies have changed significantly in recent years."[19]

Members of Congress also expressed skepticism that standards and assessments would improve schools. Without adequate resources, they maintained, many schools, particularly those in

inner cities, would never be able to bring students up to high standards of achievement. "I can predict in certain schools what the test
[results] will be by what the schools are like," said Representative
Dale E. Kildee, a Democrat from Michigan who served on the standards council. Setting off a nearly two-year battle, Kildee argued
that the only way to improve all schools is to set national school
delivery standards, not state-level standards as the NCEST report
recommended.[20]

Heeding all of these voices of caution, House Democrats effectively reined in the stampede toward national testing. In its version
of legislation drafted in response to President Bush's America 2000
proposal, the House approved the creation of the national standards
council and gave it authority to oversee the development of standards, as noted earlier; but the House prohibited any action on
assessments beyond the research-and-development stage. But while
House and Senate conferees agreed on a compromise bill, the legislation ultimately fell victim to election-year politics: Senate
Republicans killed it rather than send it to President Bush, who
would have been forced either to sign a bill he did not like or to
veto an education bill just before a presidential election.

The following year, with Bill Clinton in the White House, the
new Administration and Congress moved quickly to craft a new
school reform bill, but they, too, moved cautiously on national testing. Clinton's Goals 2000 legislation would have created a National
Education Standards and Improvement Council (the word *assessment* was removed from the council proposed by the Republicans)
and would have authorized it to certify national standards as "world
class." States, in order to qualify for improvement grants authorized
in the bill as originally worded, would have been required to
develop standards tied to the national standards and assessments
tied to their own standards. They also would have been required to
adopt standards for schools—similar to the school delivery standards envisioned in the NCEST report—to ensure that all students
have an "opportunity to learn" the content standards. But the bill

stopped short of requiring that the state assessments match the national standards, thus effectively curbing the development of a national assessment system.

In debating the proposal over the next year, House Democrats added additional provisions that would have further slowed the creation of a new assessment system. Reviving the concerns expressed by Representative Kildee from the previous year's debate, the Democrats insisted that no assessment could be used for any high-stakes purpose unless standards for students' opportunity to learn were in place. Without such a provision, the Democrats argued, it would be unfair to hold students with poorly trained teachers or crumbling facilities accountable for meeting high standards for performance. But this proposal met stiff resistance from governors and Republicans, who argued that stringent opportunity-to-learn standards would take away schools' flexibility in the issue of how to meet the performance standards.

In the end, Congress and the Administration agreed on a compromise, which President Clinton signed into law at a San Diego school in March of 1994. The law codified the national education goals and formally created the National Education Standards and Improvement Council to certify national standards. It also provided grants to states to develop reform plans that included standards for students, new assessments, and "standards or strategies" for ensuring students' opportunity to learn. The measure emphasized that the national standards would be voluntary only and that states would not be required to submit their standards and assessments to the national council for certification. However, the Administration also made state standards a key feature in its proposal to reauthorize the massive Elementary and Secondary Education Act. In order to be eligible for federal funds for Chapter I—the largest federal precollegiate education program—states must develop standards for curriculum content and student performance.

The Goals 2000 result was a disappointment to some who had argued for a national assessment system. But despite that, the legislation did in fact help create a new way of knowing what young people know, and it does so in a way that acknowledges that the technology for such a system is still evolving. As we will see, creating new assessments is proving more difficult in practice than in theory.

The legislation's most significant step toward the new system is the provision creating the new council to certify national standards. As we have seen, the federal government had issued grants to private education and research organizations to set national standards in core subject areas. These standards projects were designed to fulfill the promise started by the mathematics teachers to develop national definitions of what students ought to know and be able to do in key subjects. And like the math teachers' document, the standards projects in other subject areas call for substantial changes from current practice. If these standards are certified by the new council, those changes may come about.

Some critics of the legislation, including Diane Ravitch, who was assistant secretary of education in the Bush Administration and launched the standards projects, have lamented that the lack of a national assessment system will render the emerging standards meaningless. Since schools tend to teach what is tested, only an assessment system tied to the standards, Ravitch and others have argued, will ensure that they are implemented. But that view sells the standards short. If embraced by teachers, the standards could become the framework for revamped instruction—including new assessments, since assessments based on standards for performance are a key element of the new view of how we know what students know. But in order to change, teachers need time and support, as well as a vision to aim for. The standards provide that vision.

Another piece of the legislation that could open the door to a new way of measuring student performance is the provision authorizing the national council to certify state standards and assessments. Some critics have argued that this provision leaves authority at the state level, not at the national level, at a time when the national goals demand information on progress toward national standards. But as we have seen, states are moving to create definitions of student performance and new ways of measuring it. And there is nothing in the bill to stop them from linking their efforts in the future. Right now, research suggests that it is very difficult to link different tests to common standards, despite NCEST's hope that it can be done. Perhaps, as the technology emerges, the links will as well.

In considering the federal legislation, though, we cannot ignore the privately funded efforts to develop a national assessment system that are already under way: the College Board's Pacesetter project and the New Standards Project. Although still in the pilot stage, the projects have strong support. New Standards involves nineteen states—including the three largest (California, New York, and Texas)—and six school districts, which together enroll about half the schoolchildren in the country. And other states are clamoring to join. Perhaps when the projects are fully developed, states might want to replace their testing systems with the New Standards or Pacesetter exams; in many cases, the goals for a new way of knowing what students know are the same. But even if states opt to retain their own systems, the New Standards Project and Pacesetter could, if they prove viable, provide information on individual students' progress toward national standards—exactly what some educators and policy makers have urged since the 1989 Charlottesville summit.

But the question of whether the projects will succeed in their ambitious aims remains open. As educators and policy makers in many schools and states have found, putting in place new systems based on standards and new assessments is difficult. Like any new technology, the new systems do not always work as well in practice as they do on the drawing board. And they have met stiff resistance from people who are reluctant to give up the old ways and who are suspicious of the new. In the next chapter, we will examine some of the difficulties schools and states are encountering as they try to put the new systems in place.

Chapter Six

Between Rhetoric and Reality

The members of the Pennsylvania State Board of Education knew they were going to shake up Pennsylvania's education system in the early 1990s, but they had little idea just how explosive their plan would turn out to be.

Following two years of study, ten public hearings, and a dozen town meetings, the board met in March 1992 to consider a sweeping change in education policy. No longer would the state require students to complete a specified number of courses in order to graduate from high school, as Pennsylvania and many other states had done for years. Instead, the state would specify required "learner outcomes," and students would have to demonstrate that they had mastered the outcomes to earn a diploma.

The proposal represented perhaps the most far-reaching effort by a state to seek a new way of knowing what students know. It called for setting clear and visible standards for performance for all students and said, in essence, that the state would evaluate its students only on the basis of their demonstration of knowledge and skills. Like the high schools in Littleton, Colorado, the Pennsylvania board maintained that the existing system was inadequate because it revealed too little about what students knew and allowed students to get away with achieving too little. And to change the system, the board focused on defining the performance that all students would have to attain and assessing, in new ways, whether they had attained it.

But the plan prompted a hailstorm of protest from parents and lawmakers that made the challenge in Littleton seem tame by comparison. The protesters in Pennsylvania charged that the state board's plan would impose "values" on children and would take away from instruction in academic skills and knowledge. Although the critics did not succeed in killing the plan, their vociferous attacks sent a shudder through the spines of educators in Pennsylvania and in other states considering new standards and assessment systems. As the Pennsylvania experience illustrates, shifting to a new way of measuring student performance will not be easy or painless. In the often-contentious arena of education policy, defining what students should know—and how we know what they know—can precipitate epic battles.

But even if educators can win those battles, they also face substantial hurdles in their efforts to make sure the new instruments are sound and do in fact tell us what we need to know. Building a new way of knowing what young people know requires a new technology, and that technology is still full of uncertainties and potential pitfalls. As we will see, educators and researchers do not yet have all the answers. But despite these political and technical hurdles, educators remain convinced that shifting to a new way of measuring student performance is essential, and the movement is sure to continue.

The Battle Over Outcomes-Based Education

Like some other education skirmishes, such as the ongoing contentious battle over reading instruction, the debate on the Pennsylvania proposal to set learner outcomes burst quickly out of education circles and into a public forum. Like most states, Pennsylvania had never explicitly defined what its students should know or be able to do. High school students had to take twenty-one courses, including four years of English and three each of social studies, science, and math, but the state never spelled out what they should learn in those courses. The state did, however, administer a basic-skills test, known as the Test of Essential Learning and Literacy Skills (TELLS), which provided a traditional statement of what children know: it asked them questions for which they could choose the correct answer and then judged them in comparison with one another.

TELLS was also hotly controversial within Pennsylvania. One year, state officials ranked the 501 school districts according to their performance on the test, a move that outraged the mostly urban districts that ranked near the bottom. School officials also claimed that the state failed to follow through on a pledge to provide remedial help for students who fared poorly on the test.

Encountering these problems, the state board set off on a completely new path. Under their plan, the board would set broad standards for what students should know and be able to do, and it would create new assessments to measure students' attainment of the standards. Like the reforms in Vermont, California, and elsewhere cited earlier, the Pennsylvania plan would redefine how we know what students know. As in those states, we would know that students knew science, for example, if they could demonstrate that they understood scientific concepts, not if they scored above average on a test. The plan also envisioned inverting the heavy, top-down regulation that has traditionally governed schools. In contrast to the practice in most states, the Pennsylvania plan called for scrapping most of the rules the state had imposed on schools—rules that governed the number of courses that should be taught and the number of minutes of instruction in each subject. Instead, school districts would have the freedom to determine how to bring students up to the standards and to create their own assessments in accordance with state goals.

Originally, the board compiled a forty-five-page list of outcomes for students. By the time the panel was ready to vote on the plan, it had whittled the total down to a two-page list of about fifty-five outcomes. They included goals in nine academic areas: communications, mathematics, science and technology, environment and ecology, citizenship, arts and humanities, career education and work, wellness and fitness, and home economics. The mathematics goals, for example, would require students to (among other skills) demonstrate that they could use numbers, number systems, and equivalent forms to represent theoretical and practical situations; compute, measure, and estimate to solve theoretical and practical problems; apply the concepts of patterns, functions, and relations to solve problems; and evaluate, infer, and draw appropriate conclusions from charts, tables, and graphs.

In addition to those subject-specific goals, other goals proposed that students demonstrate that they had developed "self-worth," information and thinking skills, the ability to learn both independently and cooperatively, adaptability to change, ethical judgment, and honesty, responsibility, and tolerance.

The board's plan also called for the state to develop assessments in reading, writing, and mathematics (and to add assessments in additional subjects in the future) that would gauge the extent to which schools and school districts were enabling students to achieve and exceed the student learning outcomes. According to the plan, performance of a school on the reading assessment "shall be demonstrated by its students' responses to comprehension questions about age-appropriate reading passages and by the quality of their written responses to in-depth comprehension questions about the passages. Quality in written responses shall be judged on the basis of focus on the topic, with specific, supported, and developed details or inferences and appropriate examples from the passages." The math assessments would also require written solutions; these would be judged "on the basis of an understanding of the problem and development of methods of deriving a correct response." The plan also required the state's department of education to develop standards for "acceptable" and "excellent" levels of performance and to provide to school districts examples of student work at each of the levels.

The plan required districts to develop their own assessments as well. These could include written work, scientific experiments, works of art, teacher-made examinations, portfolios, or other measures, including standardized tests. The district-developed assessments would be used to set standards for the transition from one level of education to another—such as from elementary school to middle school—and to determine if students had attained the state-developed outcomes. In addition, students would also be required to complete a project "in one or more areas of concentrated study." The project, in research or writing, was intended to show whether students could apply, analyze, synthesize, and evaluate information and communicate their understanding.[1]

Perhaps to the surprise of board members, however, the plan met a wall of criticism. Some groups, including the Pennsylvania Federation of Teachers, the smaller of the state's two teachers' unions, questioned whether the plan left too much flexibility to local school boards. The union charged that the rules allowed boards to eliminate programs—and thus teachers—and curtail such rights as collective bargaining. The teachers also warned that the outcomes were too vague to offer any guidance to help teachers change their instruction. Unlike the detailed curriculum frameworks California produced, which (as we have seen) became the basis for new assessments, the one-sentence outcomes in Pennsylvania said little about the type of classroom practice or student performance that was expected.

But the most vocal howls of protest came from a largely right-wing group that claimed to represent "tens of thousands" of parents. When the state board met to consider the outcomes plan, more than 200 people jammed into the board's hearing room in Harrisburg and urged the panel to reject it. The critics contended that, under the plan, schools would measure students' attitudes and beliefs, not their reading and writing skills. "How do you measure someone's self-worth?" asked Peg Luksik, a former Republican candidate for governor, who helped lead the protest. "How much is enough?"[2]

The critics also questioned the need for the background information—general information about children's families and homes that might help explain test results—that state officials would collect as part of the assessment system. Although such questionnaires are a common feature of testing programs, the Pennsylvania protesters charged that the state was creating a "data base" on children and families that would violate the families' privacy.

In the wake of the protest, the board at its March 1992 meeting approved the plan but put off until September a vote on the outcomes themselves, in order to provide time for additional hearings on them. But that decision did not mollify the critics. They appealed to the legislature, where the state House, in a nonbinding vote, voiced its disapproval of the plan.

With the temperature thus raised, the issue then moved to the Independent Regulatory Review Commission, a state agency charged with overseeing all state rules. There, though, the opponents went too far. After reading briefs from critics, the chairman of the review commission indicated that he favored putting off the changes for further study. But after parent groups made their case in a hearing, he changed his mind, and the panel voted to move the plan forward.

The controversy continued when the board took up the outcomes themselves. Due in part to a warning from the chairman of the House Education Committee, who was also a member of the state board of education, that the plan faced steep opposition in the legislature, the panel put off a vote on the standards. Then Governor Robert Casey elected to intervene and asked the board to eliminate several of the proposed outcomes that had provoked controversy. However, the board adopted the set of fifty-five outcomes in November of 1992.

Again that move failed to quell the contention, and again it moved to the legislature. There critics decided to play a trump card: their supporters in the House attached an amendment to kill the entire outcomes-based system to legislation authorizing funds for special education. School districts desperately needed the special education funds, so the legislature had to come to some resolution on the outcomes. Casey again offered a compromise, and the legislature and the state board adopted it. The outcomes-based education system became law in 1993. The outcomes go into effect for the high school class of 1999.

Though nowhere has the issue been as contentious as in Pennsylvania, the shift to a new way of measuring student performance has encountered political resistance in other places as well. At times, the arguments of the critics have sounded suspiciously familiar across state lines, suggesting that a national network is behind the opposition. At a conference in Washington, D.C., in 1993, a top official from the California Department of Education heard a presentation on learning outcomes by a Pennsylvania teachers' union official and said that he thought the union officer was talking about California, not Pennsylvania. The term the Pennsylvania board used to characterize its reform, "outcomes-based education" (or OBE), has become so politically charged that states are now going to great lengths to avoid using it for fear of raising a red flag among parent groups. In Littleton, for example, school board candidates who favored the schools' reforms spent a good deal of time explaining that the changes did not represent OBE.

Wariness Over Outcomes and Judgments

In many communities, parents and community members are wary of changing the way we measure performance. They feel comfortable with the traditional method, even though, as we have seen, it does not really tell us what children know and can do. They fear that switching to a new system amounts to changing the rules of the game, which might put their children at a disadvantage when they apply to college or enter the job market. This concern is particularly acute in communities that consider their schools good; they look askance at any attempt to tamper with success, as we have seen.

Some of the resistance to the new standards and assessment systems reflects suspicion of the standards schools are proposing. To some people, a report listing abilities that a student has demonstrated sounds more fuzzy and less scientific than a report specifying that a student is in the seventy-fifth percentile, especially if the proposed outcomes represent goals for student attitudes rather than cognitive skills. Reflecting concerns from the business world and from research on learning, educators have sought to place a value on students' cooperation and attitudes toward learning, among other traits. But to parents and others accustomed to traditional classrooms, such goals represent attempts to measure—and thus mold—values that are more properly the province of families. The presence of these kinds of goals became the focus of the opposition in Pennsylvania, and the perception that OBE equaled an attempt to measure values became hard to shake even after the state, as part of the final compromise, dropped those outcomes from the list of those they would assess.

But even purely academic goals sound less rigorous than numerical targets when they are spelled out. Recall that in Littleton, Colorado, the local newspaper disparaged Mark Twain Elementary School's attempt to outline pupils' abilities, not just their letter grades, on report cards.

The wariness toward the new methods also stems in part from the fact that scoring is based on teachers' judgments, not computer scanning. As we have seen, many states and schools have enlisted teachers to score performance-based assessments and portfolios to acquaint them with the kind of instruction they want to foster and to provide them with concrete examples of high-quality student work. To score the products, teachers read the students' work and evaluate it according to agreed-upon standards. But to some, this method is too subjective.

This concern is particularly worrisome for minorities, who fear that they could be subject to biases and suffer harm if student work were evaluated on what they see as subjective grounds. After all, as some have pointed out, this shift is coming about at a time when minorities appear to be making headway on "objective" tests. Shirley Weber, the president of the San Diego school board, articulated this concern at a national conference: "When we talk about the issue of equity, the kind of assessments we're talking about require much more faith in individuals and the belief that people can actually apply equity in testing. Most of the time with a normed test you think of something that has some subjectivity in the development of the instrument, but then in the final result you know what the answer is. When you start talking about some of the assessments we're doing—portfolios—it's all subjective."[3]

In reality, as we have seen, the scoring of the new assessments is based on specific standards, and teachers receive extensive training on how to apply them. They often are unaware of the name or ethnic background of the student whose work they are evaluating. But convincing the public that this method is a valid way of knowing what young people know is a big job. Many Americans are not ready to trust teachers in that way. Teachers are, unfortunately, not held in very high esteem. They are among the lowest paid of all professionals, and many people do not consider them professionals at all. One of the reasons for the early explosion in popularity of standardized testing was the fact that computer scanners appeared to take teachers' judgment out of the equation. In order for the new assessment methods to win widespread acceptance, educators and public officials must demonstrate that the methods are valid, reliable, and fair and that they are indeed better methods of measuring students' knowledge and skills.

Technical Obstacles

These technical concerns—validity, reliability, fairness—as well as the practical concerns of cost and feasibility, have proven to be as obstructive as the political hurdles facing the new assessment methods. But scholars are just beginning to learn how the new instruments can be used to measure students' abilities. This time-lag is natural for any new technology, and tests are essentially just that—technologies for knowing what young people know. It was easy to find fault with horse-drawn carriages and propose a new kind of vehicle that would more quickly and easily take people where they wanted to go. It was much more difficult to build an automobile that would meet those demands and prove roadworthy.

But the mismatch between the demand for the new products and the supply of proven ones has caused some tension between policy makers and the research community over the issue of assessment. In an effort to produce education change quickly, various legislators and governors have embraced the promise of performance-based assessments and have mandated an immediate shift to the new instruments. When researchers initially raised their hands and expressed caution, they looked to the politicians like obstructionists; so the scholars stepped up their pace and can now report some data. But they are still building the airplane while flying it, as was noted earlier.

Critics of the restructuring effort in Littleton, Colorado, meanwhile, seized on the emerging nature of the state of the art in challenging the new system in that school district. Steeping themselves in technical literature, the three parents who ran successfully for school board seats concluded that the new forms of assessment were too experimental for use in awarding or denying students high school diplomas. The opponents claimed that although performance-based assessments had been used successfully in the classroom, as at Mark Twain, they had not yet proved themselves as measures of performance by which to hold students or schools accountable. As the critics wrote in a flyer distributed in Littleton,

> One of the reasons for concern over high-stakes uses of performance assessments is that they entail evaluations based on subjective judgments (e.g., persuasiveness, clarity, coherence, relevance, originality). It is very difficult to prove that these judgments are reasonable, fair, and unbiased!

> National assessment experts are emphatic in insisting that any
> tests used for high-stakes, life-shaping decisions must meet rigorous,
> demanding standards. . . . Are we ready to deny diplomas, and the
> educational and employment opportunities to which they provide
> access, on the basis of tests which cannot be proven to be valid and
> sound?[4]

As this statement makes clear, the technical issues are not mere
academic concerns. Only by ensuring that tests are sound can states
and schools use the instruments to hold schools and students
accountable for the results. Otherwise, in this litigious society, they
face lawsuits from students claiming that they were unfairly denied
a diploma or from schools challenging sanctions. Although the critics of the Littleton policy did not explicitly state that they would
challenge the system in court, that threat loomed not far in the
background of their challenge.

At the same time, poor technical quality compromises the education value of the assessments. We cannot know what a student
knows in math (or the strength of a school's math program) and
have any hope of improving weaknesses if the results of a math
assessment are unreliable.

To gauge the quality of assessments, members of the testing
community have come up with a number of criteria. The best
known of these are the standards for psychological and educational
testing developed by the American Educational Research Association, the American Psychological Association, and the National
Council on Measurement in Education. Last revised in 1984, the
standards are currently undergoing a new round of revision that is
expected to take into account the growing use of performance-based
assessments.

Another set of guidelines, aimed more at the "consumers" of
tests, has been developed by the National Forum on Assessment, a
coalition led by FairTest and the Council for Basic Education.

Can We Trust Test Results?

Let us turn now to the criteria that contribute to the "trustworthiness" of any given assessment.

Validity

Perhaps the most important criterion in evaluating tests is validity. Generally speaking, a test is valid if it measures what it is supposed to measure. A calendar is a valid measure of time but not a valid measure of temperature, even though it is usually colder in winter than in summer. Similarly, a test might be a valid measure of a student's mathematics achievement but not a valid measure of a school's quality, even though many schools with large numbers of high achievers are good.

The issue of validity is important in determining whether a test is appropriate for use in high-stakes circumstances. A recent court decision illustrates this. In South Carolina, the state legislature passed a law aimed at regulating home schooling—the right exercised by some parents to teach their children at home—by requiring parents to take a test to qualify as home schoolers. To carry out the law, the state's department of education selected a test that had been used to determine whether college students were eligible to enter teacher-training programs. A private firm hired by the department to validate the test for use with home schoolers determined that it was valid, so the department began testing parents. But in a case filed by parents, a state judge ruled that the validation was improper and that the test was not in fact a valid measure of parents' ability to teach their children at home. He noted, for example, that the test included questions on classroom management, which the parents contended was irrelevant to home schoolers. Although few parents had been denied permission to teach because they failed the test, the judge's ruling meant that *no* parent could be denied such permission on the basis of the test.

Advocates of new forms of assessment argue that performance measures are more likely to be valid measures of students' achievement than multiple-choice tests. Asking a student to write an essay in an effort to determine her writing ability has higher validity than asking her multiple-choice questions on grammar, since the performance test itself is close to what we really want to measure, not just an approximation of it. Moreover, scholars have expanded the definition of validity to include the consequences of testing. In other words, in evaluating whether we can draw proper inferences from test results, we must consider the test's effects on instruction. If a test leads teachers to emphasize a narrow area of content that is tested, or to spend their time and students' time on test practice materials, that test may not be a valid measure of achievement in a given subject. On that score, too, performance-based assessment appears to have the edge. As we have seen, the classroom consequences of multiple-choice testing include an overemphasis on the kinds of basic skills such tests tend to stress; classrooms using performance assessments, on the other hand, focus more on complex, real-world tasks.

In practice, though, performance-based assessments, projects, and portfolios are *not* necessarily valid measures of student achievement. A test is only a technology, and it can be used for good or ill. Teachers can narrow instruction to the type of performance demanded by a performance-based assessment just as they can teach to a multiple-choice test. And while that type of performance may be better than the mindless drill and practice students do to prepare for traditional tests, it does not necessarily lead to high levels of learning. As assessment researchers Robert L. Linn, Eva L. Baker, and Stephen B. Dunbar write, "It cannot just be assumed that more 'authentic' assessment will result in classroom activities that are more conducive to learning. We should not be satisfied, for example, if the introduction of a direct writing assessment led to greater amounts of time being devoted to the preparation of brief compositions following a formula that works well in producing highly rated essays in a twenty-minute time limit."[5]

At the same time, performance measures do not necessarily measure what they purport to measure. A performance task—say, a science experiment—may look sophisticated and appear to draw out students' abilities to think and apply scientific principles. But it may turn out that students can complete the task by memorizing formulas. Worse still, a task may be utterly baffling to students and not measure any abilities at all. It is in large part for this reason that shifting to a new way of measuring student performance will take time: the new assessments must be tried out in actual classrooms to determine exactly what they measure and whether they are indeed valid.

Some studies have raised questions about the validity of one new form of assessment: measures of students' group performance. A number of schools and states, notably Kentucky, have included in their new programs tasks for students to complete in groups, and they are evaluated, in part, on the extent to which students work together to complete each task. Collaboration is an important skill; few of us work completely on our own as adults. Yet in school, and in particular on traditional tests, we work alone at our desks. Cooperation is called "cheating."

In a series of experiments, Noreen Webb of the University of California, Los Angeles, found that group assessments may not tell us much about what individual students know. Working with seventh-grade mathematics classes in Los Angeles, Webb helped train teachers in carrying out cooperative group work in classrooms. The students organized themselves into groups of four to solve a series of math problems. To test their abilities, Webb asked the students to solve problems, such as figuring out the cost of a long-distance telephone call, in their groups. Each of the group members turned in a solution, and nearly all were correct. Webb then asked the students to solve the same problem individually, and the results were startling. Fewer than two-thirds of the students answered the questions correctly, even though they had "solved" the problem as part of the group.

What was going on? Listening to tape recordings of the group meetings, Webb found some answers. In some cases, the group work truly helped students who did not understand how to solve the problem. Their peers explained the solution to them and brought them to an understanding. But in others, the interaction appeared to have little effect. Some group members simply copied their peers' work. Others asked for help, and their peers corrected their mistakes. In still other cases, students attempted to explain the problem to group members having problems but did not do so adequately; the struggling students simply parroted their peers' explanations, and when confronted with the need to solve the problem themselves could not do so.

The experiment suggests the need for caution in using group assessments. While such instruments measure important skills—the ability to work together and to explain things to peers, for example—they may not measure the abilities of the individual members of the groups.[6]

Perhaps the most significant question about the validity of the new assessment methods is the amount of information the new assessments provide about student abilities. Multiple-choice tests typically include a large number of questions that students are expected to answer quickly. As a result, the tests can survey a broad spectrum of knowledge within a given subject area. But performance-based assessment tasks are generally aimed at probing the depth of students' understanding, not necessarily the breadth of their knowledge. And, as "authentic" tasks, they are expected to take time to complete. Thus such assessments include relatively few questions, and students are expected to answer these at length.

But can an assessment consisting of two or three science tasks tell us what students know about science? Some early research suggests that it cannot. In a study of middle school students, Richard J. Shavelson of the University of California, Santa Barbara, and his colleagues found that students' performance on science tasks—such as figuring out which paper towel absorbs the most water and determining sow bugs' preferences for various environments—varied widely, depending on the task and the way it was evaluated. As a result, Shavelson concluded, it would take at least ten tasks to determine what a student knows and can do in science. He noted that the results of the science study were similar to those found in studies of math, writing, and job-skills performance as well.[7]

Some educators are responding to findings such as Shavelson's by increasing the breadth of their assessments to ensure that they provide a valid measure of student abilities. At Mark Twain Elementary School, teachers are considering breaking up the research assessment into several smaller projects. The large project would then encompass a broad range of topics—a paper on the Civil War, for example, might reflect knowledge about the Constitution, Reconstruction, and the 1960s civil rights movement—with the smaller "chunks" helping to cover a broader range of a subject area's domain. The assessment is "a wonderful thing now," says Principal Kenneth Turner. "The large task mimics a doctoral dissertation. The child goes from ground zero, chooses the question, surveys the literature, stitches together the pieces into a presentation. The problem is, the validity challenge is real, and it needs to be taken seriously, especially if the stakes are high."[8]

Another way schools are responding to such challenges is through the use of portfolios. If increasing the number of tasks in an on-demand assessment seems prohibitively time-consuming, a portfolio of work from throughout the school year could serve the same purpose. Moreover, a portfolio, like a large-scale project, offers the benefit of allowing students and teachers, not external assessors, to determine the products on which they will be evaluated.

Reliability

A second major criterion in evaluating assessments is reliability. As the word implies, reliability indicates whether test scores can be trusted. In considering the concept, test-makers often refer to two kinds of reliability. The first is *stability*. This reflects the degree of consistency of a student's score. Do an individual student's test scores remain the same when you administer a single test on different days? The second type of reliability is *interrater reliability*, and this measures the extent to which the judges, or raters, evaluate a student's performance consistently.

Since tests gauge only estimates of a student's total knowledge and skills, no test is completely, 100 percent reliable. Test-makers express the degree of reliability through a statistical measure called a reliability coefficient. The higher the reliability coefficient—expressed as a number between 0 and 1—the more confidence one can place in the results. Yet all scores have some margin of error. On a test with high reliability, for example—one with a reliability coefficient of, say, 0.95—a student's score of 100 can mean a proficiency of anywhere from 93 to 107. Such information is often buried in statistical reports on test scores, however, and is not often public knowledge.

For a variety of reasons, standardized multiple-choice tests generally have a high degree of reliability. But they are not perfectly reliable. A student's score can vary from day to day for a host of reasons, ranging from whether she had breakfast or not to construction noise outside the classroom. Nevertheless, the *administration* of a test is consistent; that is what makes the test standardized. And with a relatively large number of questions, a multiple-choice test can help ensure that a score is not tipped by a chance misreading of one question.

Initial data on performance-based assessments, however, show that some early attempts have relatively low levels of reliability, throwing into question the quality of the information they provide on students' achievement. In Britain, for example, researchers found wide variations in the way teachers administered new performance-based assessments as part of that country's new national curriculum. In some cases, a teacher would administer a task one way in the morning and a different way in the afternoon.

The research assessment at Mark Twain Elementary School, which we saw earlier, also raises questions about reliability. Although students present their projects in a consistent form, the judges ask each student a different set of questions, depending on their topic and their presentation. Do such differences affect the scoring?

One way to correct for such potential problems is to make sure that judges score each performance on a consistent basis—that is, that the interrater reliability is high. Here, too, multiple-choice tests appear to have an advantage over performance-based assessments. Computer scanning, though not flawless, can in nearly every case provide the same score each time it reads a student's answer sheet. But what happens when teachers read students' essays or listen to their oral presentations? Could different teachers give different scores, depending on how they judge the quality of the performance? And what would that say about the results?

A study of Vermont's pioneering portfolio assessment found serious problems with interrater reliability and helped bring about changes in that state's program. Recall that in Vermont, students in fourth and eighth grades compile portfolios in writing and mathematics. Teachers evaluate the portfolios and "best pieces" culled from them on a 1-to-4 scale according to several dimensions. In writing, the portfolios are scored by students' classroom teachers; a sample number are scored a second time by teacher volunteers. In math, all of the portfolios are scored at central scoring sites.

In an independent evaluation of the first year of implementation of the program, conducted for the National Center for Research on Evaluation, Standards, and Student Testing, researchers from the RAND Institute for Education and Training found that the agreement among raters on students' scores was low in both writing and math. Although on some criteria the reliability on the portfolio scoring for individual students was higher than it was on others, in no case was reliability high. However, statewide average scores were quite reliable, because of the large numbers of students involved. As a result, the researchers recommended against reporting any results below the state level.

What went wrong? The RAND researchers identified three possible reasons for the low levels of interrater agreement, and state officials moved quickly to address them. First, they pointed out that the scoring systems could help cause some of the errors in scoring. In contrast to other performance-based assessments, in which raters generally apply a single score to a performance or portfolio, Vermont raters were originally asked to provide five separate scores in writing and seven separate scores in math. Thus math raters had to keep in mind twenty-eight scale points—four each for the seven dimensions. Moreover, the researchers suggested, different teachers could have interpreted the scoring guide differently, with some looking for how frequently a student uses a particular technique and others scoring on the basis of the quality of a student's techniques.

The report also suggested that inadequate training may have contributed to low levels of reliability. Like many alternative assessment programs, the Vermont program was intended both to improve instruction and to provide information on student performance. To accomplish these twin goals, the state invited all teachers to participate in the scoring so that as many teachers as possible could take advantage of the professional development such scoring provides. But the state could not guarantee that all teachers were equally well trained in applying the scoring guides.

A third possible reason for the low levels of reliability, according to the RAND report, related to the portfolio program itself. Unlike performance tasks, in which students answer the same questions, portfolios include a wide variety of materials prepared in response to quite different classroom assignments. Because teachers scoring the portfolios had no "anchor" on which to tie their scoring, they may have veered off from side to side.[9]

Responding to the report, Vermont officials introduced several changes in their program. They eliminated one suggested type of math problem, which proved difficult to score. They considered adding a standard item to serve as an anchor. And they assigned the task of scoring portfolios for the statewide results to a group of highly trained raters; however, they insisted that any Vermont teacher could become—and should try to become—part of that elite group. Yet the state refused to back away from its intention to find a new way of knowing what its students know. Officials felt confident that the problems could be solved. Indeed, the next year's results showed improvement. There was much greater reliability in the math scores, although the scoring of the writing continued to exhibit problems.

Fairness

In addition to validity and reliability, tests are also judged on the basis of fairness. Because of civil rights concerns, tests can be subject to litigation if they unfairly disadvantage members of a racial or ethnic group. To alleviate such concerns, tests regularly undergo "bias reviews."

Performance assessments are no less susceptible than multiple-choice tests to bias; in fact, some argue that they are more so, since they tend to include fewer questions. One source of bias is the background knowledge questions assume. If a test includes many questions, it can tap a broad range of background knowledge; thus a student who does not know the subject of one question may find another question that represents his experience. But an assessment that includes only one or two performance tasks may place a student with limited background knowledge at a disadvantage. Consider a task that asks students to choose a pinch hitter based on batters' performance against the pitchers on the opposing team. Such a task taps a range of mathematical skills, including data analysis and computation, and it shows students how mathematics is used in the real world. But those who know little or nothing about baseball would be at a severe disadvantage.

The issue of students' background knowledge also raises questions about how to evaluate projects and portfolios. Unless schools provide clear guidelines or restrictions, students with extensive resources at home could produce better products than those with less ready access to encyclopedias or other books. Perhaps more serious, schools must be watchful for help from knowledgeable family members. While schools may want to encourage parents to discuss their children's schoolwork with them, they do not want parents to actually do the assignments.

Another potential source of bias in tests is the content knowledge and skills that the questions assume. This may not seem prejudicial, since tests are *supposed* to measure academic knowledge and skills (and the closer they reflect actual coursework, the better they are at measuring what children know and can do). But if there are differences in instruction from school to school, the assessments may be more a measure of school curricula than of student abilities. This is not necessarily a bad thing; we want to know what schools are teaching so that we can suggest changes if necessary. And the goal of many of the new assessment programs is to make the standards explicit for students so that they can strive for high levels of performance. But if we decide to place consequences on the results of an assessment, we must know whether students were aware of the standards upon which they would be judged and whether they had the opportunity to learn the desired content. Otherwise, students may be held accountable for circumstances over which schools, not they, had control. As we will see, this concern has dominated congressional debate over testing policy.

At least for now, though, the effects of instruction on assessment results appear to place low-income and minority students at a disadvantage. As we have seen, such students are more likely to encounter rote drilling and test-preparation practices and are less likely to learn the kind of complex thinking and problem-solving skills that performance-based assessments attempt to tap. As a result, schools that have implemented new assessments without completely transforming instruction have found that the gap between advantaged and disadvantaged students appears to have widened.

One striking piece of evidence illustrating this problem comes from the National Assessment of Educational Progress. In its 1992 math assessment, NAEP included questions that asked students to construct their own responses to complex problems—five questions on its fourth-grade test and six each on its eighth- and twelfth-grade tests. These questions were added in an attempt to bring the assessment more in line with the standards for math instruction developed by the National Council of Teachers of Mathematics. Although NAEP provided a relatively short period of time for students to answer these questions—the entire test takes only an hour to complete—the extended-response questions did offer a new way of measuring student performance.

The results were dramatic. Overall performance on the new questions was poor—much worse than performance on traditional multiple-choice questions. But among African American students and those from low-income families, the results were particularly disturbing. Only 5 percent of African American fourth-graders answered the extended-response questions satisfactorily or better, compared with 20 percent of the white fourth-graders. By contrast, African Americans answered 38 percent of the multiple-choice questions correctly, compared with 53 percent for whites. The gap was wider when looked at by socioeconomic group. Among fourth-graders from "advantaged urban areas"—generally suburbs—26 percent answered the extended-response questions satisfactorily or better, while only 5 percent of those from "disadvantaged urban areas"—largely inner cities—provided satisfactory responses to such questions. On multiple-choice questions, by contrast, the advantaged fourth-graders answered 59 percent correctly, while those from disadvantaged areas got 39 percent right.[10]

New assessments may also place those with limited proficiency in English at a disadvantage. Asking students to demonstrate what they know and are able to do has usually meant asking them to write. For example, math assessments ask students to explain their answers as a way of demonstrating their ability to communicate their understanding. But a student new to this country and to the English language may have less facility in writing than one who was born here. In that case, a poor performance on the math assessment could indicate more of a problem with writing ability than with knowledge of math. Such concerns helped prompt California officials to include in the new California Learning Assessment System opportunities for students to respond with figures and graphics as well as words. But as teachers in Vermont indicated in their responses to the RAND survey, many educators remain wary of judging students' math abilities on the basis of written responses.

Another source of potential bias in the new assessments relates to the use of curriculum materials. As part of an effort to ensure that reading assessments measure comprehension ability, several of the new programs include actual literature, as we have seen, not just passages created for the test. States try to keep the names of the stories secret, so that no one will read them in preparation for the assessment. But some students may have read them already, in class or for leisure, and they will have an unfair advantage over those seeing them for the first time.

Performance Standards: How Good Is Good Enough?

As they build the new "airplanes," the pathfinders in the search for new ways of knowing what young people know must also be sure that the standards for student performance are sound. Otherwise, the reports of the results will lose credibility. Who can believe that few students attained the top level of performance if the definition of the top level is suspect?

The attempt by the National Assessment Governing Board (NAGB) to set standards for student performance on the National Assessment of Educational Progress is illustrative of the problems that might arise in standards-setting. The board, a twenty-four-member panel of public officials, educators, and representatives of the general public, was created by Congress in 1988 as an independent policy-setting authority for the project. (In the past, policies had been set by an arm of the organization that conducted the assessment under contract to the U.S. Education Department; since 1983, the contractor has been the Educational Testing Service, the nation's largest testing firm.) In one of its first acts, the panel chose to set "appropriate achievement goals" for the assessment, one of the responsibilities Congress charged the board with in the 1988 legislation that created the panel.

Board members said that the achievement goals would improve the quality of the information NAEP provided by comparing students' performance to agreed-upon standards for achievement rather than to other students' performance (as the assessment had done since its inception). As Chester E. Finn, Jr., the former assistant U.S. secretary of education and chairman of the governing board, put it, the new method would indicate "how good is good enough."[11] Thus, although NAEP is a fairly traditional test, with multiple-choice questions removed from everyday classroom work, the achievement goals would move the project closer to the new ideas of how to measure student performance.

Following several public hearings, and after some modifications, the board in May of 1990 approved the plan to set achievement levels for NAEP. (Board members changed the name from achievement *goals* to avoid confusion with the national education goals adopted by President Bush and the nation's governors earlier that year.) Under their plan, mentioned briefly in the previous chapter, the board would report the proportion of students who performed at basic, proficient, and advanced levels on the assessment. According to the board's definition, the proficient level was the key: it indicated solid grade-level performance. Those at the basic level demonstrated partial mastery of needed skills and knowledge, while those at the advanced level demonstrated exceptional achievement. The board agreed to try out the new system on the 1990 mathematics assessment, which had been administered the previous spring. That assessment was noteworthy, because it was the first to include state-by-state results.

To set the standards, NAGB (pronounced *nag-bee)* invited sixty-three teachers, school administrators, business and military officials, and mathematics educators to Vermont for two days. Using a variation of a common procedure in testing, the group examined test questions to determine whether students at the basic, proficient, and advanced levels of achievement, according to NAGB's definitions, should be able to answer them. When participants were unable to complete the procedure, the board invited them to reconvene in Washington, D.C., to finish their ratings (though not all were able to make the second meeting). Their results were then compiled, and a small group of educators translated them into written definitions of what students at each level of achievement should know and be able to do.

This standards-setting process prompted a tidal wave of criticism. Some objections came from educators, who questioned the need for national standards for student performance. But the most ardent critics were technical experts, who maintained that the procedure NAGB had used was seriously flawed. In a series of blistering reports, the critics—who included an independent panel of reviewers hired by NAGB to evaluate the process—found severe problems of validity and reliability that cast doubt on the results. They recommended not reporting the results unless changes were made.

Conceding some of the critics' points, but vowing to go ahead with the project, NAGB conducted what it called "validation and replication" studies. Essentially, the panel convened additional groups, consisting primarily of teachers, to conduct the same exercise the Vermont/Washington group had gone through. The board then decided to use the results from the replication studies—in other words, to indicate how well the test-takers fared against the new standards—in reporting the 1990 math assessment results.

The replication procedure failed to assuage the critics. In a draft of its final report, the independent three-person panel of reviewers hired by NAGB contended that the achievement levels were still flawed and accused NAGB of continuing the process for political reasons: to show that U.S. education is in bad shape. The board responded by firing the reviewers and went ahead and released the results, which were also included in the first annual report card on the national education goals. The results did indeed show that math performance was in bad shape. Only about 20 percent of students, according to the report, attained the proficient level, while as many as two-thirds failed to reach even the basic level of achievement.

Still committed to the achievement-level process, the board agreed that the new method should be the primary means of reporting all future NAEP results, and board members hired American College Testing (ACT), the publishers of a widely used college admissions test, to conduct the process in 1992. ACT instituted a number of changes to improve the technical quality of the standards-setting process, but a number of experts maintained that it was nevertheless flawed. The U.S. General Accounting Office, in a 1993 report, concluded that NAGB's approach yielded "misleading interpretations" of the performance of U.S. students and recommended that the board scrap the process and consider alternatives. Separately, the National Academy of Education, an honorary society of scholars and educators, concluded that the procedure NAGB used was "fundamentally flawed" and proposed some alternative standards-setting methods. As part of its analysis, the academy commissioned separate studies to examine the validity of the NAGB achievement levels and found that reports based on those levels may have seriously understated the performance of American students. The studies, in which teachers applied NAGB's definitions to student test results, found that in nearly every case, many more students appeared to attain the proficient and advanced levels than NAGB's reports indicated.[12]

This dispute over achievement levels may seem technical and arcane, but as the National Academy of Education's study shows, the implications are serious. The purpose of testing is to tell us what young people know and can do. But if the process is flawed, the information we get about student abilities becomes cloudy. Unfortunately, the caveats pointing out the problems and limitations of the information are often buried in footnotes or appendixes to reports on student achievement, and most people reading news accounts of the reports will never know about the limitations. As a result, they may take the information as literal truth when in fact it could be wrong. This, too, could have serious consequences. If schools or public agencies base education or spending policy on the "fact" that only 20 percent of students are proficient in mathematics, when in reality many more students may be at that level, their policies may be misguided. Or worse, as the National Academy report suggests, the technical flaws could destroy the credibility of the testing program. If no one believed the information such a program provided, the entire operation would be a waste. And that would be a tragedy. We need to know what young people know and can do, and setting standards for performance offers the chance of a better way of knowing—but only if the resulting information is credible, valid, and reliable.

Time and Money

While the technical concerns of validity, reliability, and fairness have led educators to move cautiously in developing new methods of measuring student performance, other concerns also loom. Two of the most important are cost and efficiency. There is no question that multiple-choice testing is the least expensive way to measure student performance and that any alternative—performance assessments, projects, or portfolios—will cost considerably more. Because there are few alternative assessments in place on a large scale, however, estimates of their costs are hard to come by.

One analysis of a large urban school district's expenditures on testing shows how inexpensive traditional tests are. Examining the total costs, both direct and indirect, related to testing in a 191,000-pupil district, the Office of Technology Assessment concluded that total annual outlays for testing were $1.6 million, or $11.40 per pupil. That included expenditures for materials, contracted scoring and reporting services, and nonteaching personnel, including researchers and administrative staff. Add to that the cost in teachers' time, or an estimated $3.6 million for administering tests, and the total comes to $5.2 million, or about $37 per pupil tested. That represents a small fraction of the district's overall budget of $1.2 billion, or $6,300 per pupil. However, the OTA also noted that the 4,500 teachers in the district reported spending anywhere from no time to three weeks preparing students for the test. Adding their time for preparation would increase the cost of the program by as much as $30 million a year—still a small item in the total.[13]

A study by the General Accounting Office provided an even lower estimate of the cost of multiple-choice tests: $16 per pupil, including the cost of the test and staff time. The GAO's finding was based on a lower estimate of the amount of time devoted to testing. According to the GAO study, the average student spends only seven hours a year on testing, including preparation, test-taking, and related activities.

Both agencies estimated that performance-based assessments would cost considerably more than multiple-choice tests, although they disagreed over the magnitude of the difference. The GAO, citing comparisons from states with both types of testing, estimated that performance assessments would cost twice as much, or $33 per pupil. The OTA, by contrast, cited studies suggesting that performance assessment could cost from three to ten times as much as multiple-choice testing.[14]

The reason for the higher cost is obvious. Scoring essays and other student performances is considerably more labor-intensive than checking marks on an answer sheet. As we have seen, states that employ the new assessment methods bring teachers together for days at a time for training and scoring. The teachers receive payment for their time and are usually compensated for travel, lodging, and meals. If the scoring takes place during the school year, their schools must provide substitute teachers to take over their classrooms while they are away. Multiple-choice tests, by contrast, can be scanned in seconds by computers, at a cost of pennies per exam.

Moreover, as the RAND Corporation study of the Vermont program showed, the new forms of assessment demand a considerable investment in classroom time. In contrast to a traditional test, which students may complete in an hour or two, students may spend several days completing a performance task (such as those on the California state assessment) or compiling problems to place into a portfolio. Teachers feeling pressure to cover all the material in a year-long course may see the time spent on such problems as intrusive. In Great Britain, teachers' frustrations with the amount of time spent on national examinations erupted in a national boycott in 1993, which led government officials to cut the amount of time spent administering the exams in half.

But as educators involved with new assessment programs are quick to point out, the tasks themselves are valuable learning experiences for students. And the time spent by teachers in administering and scoring the assessments is equally valuable. The scoring sessions for the new assessments produce a lot more than test scores. Teachers involved in scoring learn the state's standards and expectations for students. They can take back to the classroom a sense of the type of activities they ought to be offering their students. And they see examples of high-quality work to which they can compare their own students' performance. These results provide some of the best professional development teachers can have. Thus these new assessments offer benefits that traditional tests do not. And while it is true that conventional tests cost less, critics who see those tests as providing little information about what students know and can do ask what their low cost buys. To determine the value of new assessments, policy makers must consider the benefits as well as the costs.

Down to Earth

While the political and technical hurdles have slowed the shift to the new systems of measuring student performance, these obstacles have not stopped it. Educators and policy makers remain convinced that standards and new forms of assessment are the way to go. And slowing down the process has helped make the standards and assessments better. Although some of the critics of the Pennsylvania outcomes-based system continue to object to it, the delay caused by public comment, and the changes brought about by that comment, helped bring more people on board. The current list of outcomes is surely closer to a consensus on what students ought to know and be able to do than the original forty-five-page list.

At the same time, those raising technical concerns have worked to ensure that the new assessments function as intended—that they help rather than harm students. While critics of the Littleton system harbored serious doubts about the skills and knowledge the assessments measured, they focused their objections on using the unproven assessments to make judgments about students. Just as the federal Food and Drug Administration demonstrates that drugs are safe and effective before allowing them on the market, the testing experts want to show that tests measure student abilities properly and do not impede learning. Indeed, some have argued for some form of regulatory agency similar to the FDA to monitor testing. Others have called for "educational impact statements," like the environmental impact statements required for development projects, to gauge the effects of a test or other educational intervention. While neither of these proposals has yet gotten off the ground, the growing body of research literature has helped those in charge of putting the new systems in place remain aware of the limitations and potential pitfalls.

Perhaps the most important effect of the heightened scrutiny of the new standards and assessments has been to bring expectations for them back down to earth. In the early years of the movement, advocates of alternative assessments portrayed them as key levers for improving education. This vision proved appealing to public officials, particularly since testing is a relatively inexpensive way to fix schools. As Grant Wiggins, one of the leading advocates of alternative assessments, put it, "It's wrong to say [performance assessments] were oversold; they were overbought."[15]

Over the past few years, however, more and more educators and public officials have recognized that, as Wiggins said, standards and assessments are only one piece of the school reform puzzle—albeit the central and most critical piece. Making sure that all students achieve at high levels means that curriculum has to change, teaching has to change, teacher education has to change, and school organization has to change. One of the most forceful advocates of the new performance-based systems, Governor Roy Romer, uses the analogy of a sandwich to explain how education reform should work. Standards and assessments are the bread; they provide structure and shape to the enterprise. But the "meat" is what goes on in the classroom. Without a beefed-up curriculum and instruction, there is no nutrition.

In the next chapter, we will examine the daunting task that lies before reformers and see how the "bread" can—and must—play a central role in the effort.

Chapter Seven

Toward an Agenda for Reform

In the end, the school board election in Littleton, Colorado, came down to one issue: What should students know and be able to do? The two sides wrapped their arguments in discussions of the technical merits of tests, parent involvement in schools, and other concerns. But the fundamental question over which they differed is really the question of what we expect of schools. It is a question that cuts to the heart of the education enterprise, and one that is at the center of the shift to the focus on student performance: what should students know and be able to do, and how should we measure whether they have attained that knowledge and those skills?

The critics may have won the battle and dealt a setback to the movement toward a new way of knowing what young people know, but the movement continues. From Vermont to California, in schools and statehouses and in the halls of Congress, educators and public officials are becoming convinced that all students must learn at high levels and that new ways of knowing what they know are essential. This is not because schools are "failing" or because traditional practices do not work. As a number of analysts have pointed out, by a variety of measures, students today are achieving at least as well as their older brothers and sisters and their parents.

But like the Littleton reformers, the advocates of new standards and assessments recognize that soon it will no longer be good enough to succeed on the same terms as before. As we have seen, the changes in the economy, coupled with new understandings of how children learn, demand that all students attain higher levels of learning—levels tapped by new forms of assessment. And equity demands that we no longer tolerate a society in which such abilities are reserved for the few.

Yet, as the Littleton election suggests, the idea that all students should be able to reason and think critically is a radical notion. The types of problem-solving and communication abilities the designers of the new systems envision are far removed from what most schools have traditionally stressed, and they are far from what most schools continue to emphasize. The results of early efforts to implement new assessments—in Kentucky, for example, where even students in traditionally high-performing schools failed to reach the proficient level of achievement—bear this out in dramatic fashion. Thus even places that have set new goals for student performance and have developed new methods for measuring whether students have attained the goals are a long way away from their targets.

The task of raising the level of student achievement, moreover, is a huge one. It involves transforming the teaching and learning that goes on every day in every classroom in every one of the 80,000 public schools in the country. As the saying goes, the only thing that matters in education is what happens when the teacher closes the door to her classroom. Or, as officials in the Clinton Administration say, paraphrasing a slogan from the presidential campaign, "It's the classroom, stupid."

What is the best way to change what happens in the classroom to bring about high levels of learning for all? That is still a matter of heated debate. But there is near-universal agreement that the first step is setting standards and creating assessments to match them.

In the examples we have seen, the new way of measuring student performance has become the keystone of the reform edifice. Recall that at Littleton High School, for example, the new standards shaped everything in the school, from the way classrooms were organized to the types of professional-development activities teachers sought. Teachers' conversations revolved around student performance, and their practices changed accordingly. The standards and new assessments also served as a powerful impetus for teachers to change their practices, even without high stakes attached. Vermont's portfolio assessment created what Commissioner Rick Mills called a "professional-development industry"; teachers clamored to join networks to learn new methods of instruction and see the kind of student work they should foster.

Some have argued that each school should set its own standards, since the collaboration involved in the process is a valuable way to improve instruction. Indeed, as we saw at Littleton High School, the standards-setting process promoted conversations among teachers that had never occurred before. But allowing each school to go its own way would probably be ineffective and might exacerbate inequities among schools. The schools mentioned here that have moved to the forefront in shifting to a new way of knowing what young people know are in many ways exceptional. They are blessed with strong, visionary leaders and committed staff members, and in many cases they have secured additional funds to help them along their way. Not all schools are equipped well enough to move at the same pace, and it is likely that the schools that have traditionally lagged behind would be the ones that would continue to do so if each school were left to change on its own. To ensure equity, therefore, standards should be set at the state level, with the emerging national standards serving as touchstones. In fact, this is what is happening, and the Clinton Administration's Goals 2000 reform bill should give the effort a boost.

To some, the state's role should end there. According to that view, the road to high levels of student performance is relatively straightforward: set standards, develop new assessments to measure performance against the standards, and loosen regulations to allow schools to design their own method of bringing students up to the standards. Then publicize the assessment results—and in some cases provide rewards for success and penalties for failure—and schools will have an incentive to change. Indeed, some have argued that performance standards could create new *legal* standards that would allow those in low-performing schools to take school districts and states to court on the grounds that they were denied their right to a high level of educational attainment.

But one need only glance through Jonathan Kozol's searing book *Savage Inequalities* to conclude that the outcomes-based strategy alone is unfortunately unrealistic. The schools he describes in East St. Louis, Chicago, Camden, and New York City are so decrepit that it strains belief to think that moral suasion from published test scores or the possibility of legal redress on behalf of low-performing students could enable such schools to help students achieve at high levels. It is difficult to imagine students showing proficiency in carrying out a science experiment when they are shivering in drafty classrooms beneath dripping pipes—not to mention lacking laboratory facilities.[1]

And while Kozol's examples are extreme, gross inequities are sadly pervasive throughout the country. Courts in state after state have found that the disparities in school spending between wealthy and poor communities violate the constitutional mandate to provide thorough and efficient education. And while money is not the only answer, it is only fair to ensure that all students have an opportunity to learn the content the new assessments demand. Schools suffering from inequities that hamper students' opportunity to learn should not be punished for failing to educate students to high standards. Even less should students in such schools be penalized if the schools are not providing sufficient opportunity.

The issue of standards for schools (rather than or in addition to standards for students) to measure students' opportunity to learn has sparked a loud clash at the national level.

The idea of measuring students' opportunity to learn is not new, although it has been confined largely to academic circles until recently. As early as the 1960s, with the first international studies of student achievement, researchers began to discuss ways to determine whether students had been taught the material on standardized tests. The need for such information was obvious. Without it, comparisons between nations with vastly different education systems would not make sense. How could we say whether Japanese students were doing better than Americans if we did not know what students in the two countries had learned in school? Differences in performances on a test may reflect differences in *what* students were taught as well as *how well* they were taught.

The power inherent in information on students' opportunity to learn became apparent in 1987, with the release of a report on an international study of mathematics achievement. The report garnered headlines with its finding that U.S. students performed near the bottom of the international rankings. But what was most significant was why. In analyzing the differences among countries, the report found that *typical* explanations for the poor performance of U.S. youths—large class sizes, a shorter school year—did not account for the differences in math achievement among the countries in the study. What did explain the differences was the curriculum—students' opportunity to learn. The United States, the report's authors concluded, has an "underachieving curriculum" in mathematics. That conclusion provided strong support for efforts by the National Council of Teachers of Mathematics to revamp the math curriculum in schools. And those efforts, which led to the first set of national standards for school curricula, had a strong influence on similar activities by educators in other subject areas.[2]

The type of information that led to the international study's conclusion was relatively simple. Along with the test administered to students, the researchers included a survey of teachers that asked whether they had taught particular topics covered by the test and had introduced particular types of questions. Few school officials collect such information, easily accessible though it is. In a survey of large urban school districts, Floraline I. Stevens, a researcher at the National Center for Education Statistics, found only two that gathered data on students' opportunity to learn.[3]

The growing interest in standards and new forms of assessment heightened attention to the opportunity-to-learn issue. Members of the New Standards Project, the consortium of states and school districts developing a national system of examinations based on high standards for performance, pledged to adhere to a "social compact" to ensure that all students had a fair opportunity to meet the high standards. Without such an assurance, members argued, the project would unfairly set a high bar that disadvantaged students could not hurdle.

Similarly, as we saw in Chapter Five, the National Council on Education Standards and Testing, the congressionally mandated panel charged with examining the desirability and feasibility of national standards and assessments, recommended (in its 1992 report) setting "school delivery standards" to accompany curriculum and student performance standards. Like the New Standards participants, members of NCEST argued that it would be unfair to hold students to demanding standards if their schools did not provide adequate curricula and instruction.

Within NCEST, however, the idea of standards for schools proved hotly controversial, as we have seen. Governors and members of the Bush Administration objected that the proposal could turn the federal government into a "national school board" that would dictate to local schools the number of books they must keep in their libraries and the credentials of their teachers. Such mandates, they argued, represented a step backward at a time when research and good practice concurred that schools should have more, not less, flexibility in how they operate and that states should set broad targets for student performance. Not incidentally, the delivery standards also threatened to be costly if states were found liable for failing to meet them. After heated debate and an even split among members, the panel arrived at the compromise mentioned briefly earlier: although curriculum and student performance standards would be set at the national level, states could select their school delivery standards from among standards developed collectively.

In part, the battle over the opportunity-to-learn standards reflected confusion over terminology. While people could envision standards for course content and student performance, few people had an idea of what standards for students' opportunity to learn might look like. And what some people saw they did not like. To critics, a countrywide set of standards could end up becoming a national version of accreditation standards or a checklist of school characteristics (student-teacher ratios and library holdings, for example) that are at best irrelevant; at worst, they lock schools into numerical boxes and restrict their ability to make needed changes.

But just as new assessments do not resemble traditional standardized tests, opportunity-to-learn standards do not have to follow the model of accreditation standards. We could develop new ways of measuring schools that would promote equity and not stifle creativity just as we are developing ways of measuring student performance that foster, not impede, learning.

Some educators have attempted to flesh out what such standards might look like. In a report prepared for the New York State Education Department, Linda Darling-Hammond, the co-director of the National Center on Restructuring Education, Schools, and Teaching at Teachers College, Columbia University, outlines a set of "standards of practice for learner-centered schools." Like standards for student performance, which state that all students should demonstrate certain levels of ability, the standards of practice state that all schools should provide the resources and instruction to enable students to meet the standards for performance. For example, they state that all students should have access to necessary school funding; that all students should have access to well-prepared, fully qualified teachers; and that all students should have access to a rich and challenging curriculum. The report suggests that the state collect data on schools' progress toward the standards of practice and report the results just as it would report the results of student performance.

Jennifer O'Day and Marshall S. Smith have also outlined what they consider appropriate school delivery standards to accompany standards for curriculum content and student performance. Under their proposal, schools would gauge resources (such as teachers' and administrators' ability to teach challenging content), practice (such as the evidence of high-quality pedagogy), and performance.[4]

In addition to coming up with definitions of standards for schools, researchers and school officials have been developing other ways to measure whether students have had the opportunity to learn challenging content. Perhaps the simplest way to gauge that opportunity would be to study transcripts, which indicate courses taken. But transcripts in fact say very little about the type of learning experiences students have had. Courses with the same name vary widely from school to school (and even within schools). That is one reason that schools such as Littleton and Heritage High Schools proposed scrapping rules that required students to sit through four years of "mathematics" and asking them instead to demonstrate what they have learned.

In keeping with the history of the opportunity-to-learn concept, some of the most promising work is coming from researchers involved in an international study of mathematics and science achievement. As part of that study, which is the largest effort of its kind ever undertaken, curriculum experts from participating nations are examining commonly used textbooks and curriculum materials to determine whether the students tested have had the opportunity to learn the material included on a cross-national test.

In a separate experiment, California officials included in the new California Learning Assessment System questions designed to determine whether students are being taught in ways that help them answer the kind of performance exercises the program emphasizes. On the answer sheet, students are asked if they have studied open-ended questions like those on the assessment during their classroom work. Teachers are asked similar questions in a questionnaire.

Those kinds of surveys, though, are problematic. Students do not always know what they are supposed to have been taught, and teachers often respond with "socially desirable" answers that indicate what they think they should say, not what they actually did. So to provide a deeper understanding of students' opportunity to learn, researchers at the National Center for Research on Evaluation, Standards, and Student Testing have been studying actual classroom "artifacts"—assignments, homework, and tests—to gauge the kind of instruction students are exposed to. Such studies are time-consuming and expensive and can be carried out in only a small number of classrooms. But they provide an important check on the accuracy of the large-scale surveys.

Another measurement tool that has attracted favor is the British "inspectorate" system, mentioned earlier. Under that system, teams of observers spend a considerable amount of time examining the teaching and learning that goes on in schools. The inspectors lack any kind of enforcement power beyond the ability to publicize their findings. Their most important function is to enable teachers and administrators to examine their own practices with an eye toward improving them. In this country, the Coalition of Essential Schools, a network of reform-minded high schools, has adopted a variation of the inspectorate system: outside educators serve as "critical friends" of the coalition schools. In a separate project, the New York State Education Department invited David Green, one of Her Majesty's Inspectors, to develop a variation of the British system in that state. Under the New York project (known as the School Quality Review initiative), which is now being tested in a handful of schools, teams of teachers and university professors intensively study a school for a week at a time, bearing in mind the state's learning goals for students; and they produce a confidential report for the school's internal use. The idea is to replace the traditional monitoring function, in which officials go down a checklist to ensure that schools are following rules, with a system that helps schools keep their focus where it ought to be—on teaching and learning.

In time, students' portfolios could also serve the purpose of gauging schools' instructional performance. Depending on the types of materials included in the portfolios, the tools could provide an important window on the classroom that currently is closed. We could see, for example, if differences in students' reading performance reflected the fact that one group's reading assignments included great works of literature while another included rather low-level material. However it is gathered, such information is essential if all students are to have a fair shot at meeting high standards for performance.

But while the standards for schools are vital, they should not become an excuse to put off setting standards for student performance or developing new assessments. Just as we cannot expect all students to attain high standards right away, we should also not expect all schools to meet the standards at first. Postponing student standards and assessments until all students have an opportunity to learn challenging content is waiting for a day that may never arrive. Many of the inequities in our education system are the result of poverty, and while schools can alleviate some of the effects of poverty, they cannot eliminate them. Too many children, for the foreseeable future, will continue to come to school hungry and return along unsafe streets to homes without books or parents who can help them with their schoolwork. But the worst thing that could happen for those children is for schools to lower standards or expectations for them. And that is what is happening now; that is why children from low-income homes continue to lag behind their more affluent peers. Schools expect less from poor children—classrooms with a preponderance of such children, as we have seen, tend to rely on traditional tests—and they attain lower levels of achievement. But the education literature is replete with examples that demonstrate that all students, particularly those from low-income and minority backgrounds, thrive when the expectations for them are high. Thus both sets of standards—those for students and those for schools—are necessary.

They are not, however, sufficient to ensure high levels of learning. Despite the positive move toward standards for performance and new methods of assessments, states continue to send schools messages, through layer upon layer of laws and regulations, that conflict with their ambitious aims. In order to ensure that schools move toward meeting the new standards, states must make sure that all of their policies—from textbook adoption to teacher licensure—support, not impede, their aims. This kind of alignment, known in policy circles as "systemic reform," is difficult to achieve, however. Legislators and bureaucrats accustomed to thinking of particular programs or projects find it difficult to view the system as a whole.

But even if it can be achieved, systemic reform is only part of the answer. For one thing, other actors outside the state's policy reach, such as business and higher education, must also be brought in line. If colleges continue to use traditional means to admit students, and businesses decline to evaluate students' school performance in hiring, then students and schools will receive mixed messages.

Moreover, the policy levers at the disposal of statehouses, even if pulling in the same direction, are not strong enough to build the capacity of every school. What is needed is an enormous effort to transform the way teachers teach. David Cohen, a professor of education at Michigan State University, provides a vivid illustration of the depth of the changes that are needed. In an article entitled "Revolution in One Classroom (or Then Again, Was It?)," Cohen describes the case of a second-grade teacher from California he refers to as "Mrs. Oublier." Mrs. O, as he calls her, enthusiastically embraced the reform ideas in that state's curriculum framework in mathematics, which emphasizes problem solving and communication rather than calculation. She read the relevant documents and attended workshops to try to learn new methods that reflected the framework, and then she attempted to implement the ideas in her classroom. But Cohen, who observed her classes, found that she did not in fact change her instruction much at all. Although she cloaked her lessons in the trappings of reform, her goals for student learning were pretty much like those she had had before. He writes,

If the recent reforms are to succeed, students and teachers must not simply absorb a new "body" of knowledge. Rather, they must acquire a new way of thinking about knowledge and a new practice of acquiring it. They must cultivate strategies of problem solving that seem to be quite unusual among adult Americans. They must learn to treat knowledge as something they construct, test, and explore, rather than as something they accumulate. Additionally, and in order to do all of the above, they must un-learn much of what they know, whether they are second graders or veteran teachers.[5]

As difficult as the transformation is for teachers such as Mrs. O, who support education reform, it is many times greater for the rest of the more than two million teachers currently in classrooms. Many teachers are quite comfortable with their methods and are reluctant to change, particularly to methods that demand considerably more time and effort than simply following along in a textbook and administering tests off the shelf. But even if they are willing to change, many lack the wherewithal to do so. Consumed by their day-to-day responsibilities, many teachers never attend conferences or visit other schools to learn about other practices or methods. Seldom do teachers observe their colleagues within their own buildings! Moreover, providing such opportunities for teachers is expensive. At the least, schools must pay for substitutes when a teacher is away at a conference or school visit. And many school districts and states have to also pay the expenses for teachers to make such visits, since teachers cannot generally afford to pay their own way. In tight budget times, such funds may be hard to come by.

In many of the new systems of standards and/or assessment that we have looked at in these pages, though, school officials have placed a high priority on teachers' professional development. In Vermont, for example, a substantial portion of the budget for the new assessment system was devoted to professional development, and teachers clamored for the opportunities it provided. There and elsewhere, teachers have been involved in developing and scoring the assessments to familiarize themselves with the standards for student performance. Such efforts, while essential, are not enough. Many times the number of teachers who have been involved thus far in the programs must also be reached. But the programs themselves offer a big boost by providing an incentive for teachers to take advantage of the opportunities that exist. Although teachers may resent being pushed to change, these efforts do provide a powerful motivation.

But while the retraining of the teacher corps is a vital element in the reform effort, an equally important step is the reform in the teaching of beginning teachers. It is a truism that teachers teach the way they were taught. It seems obvious, then, that the best way to ensure that teachers are able to teach in the ways we expect is to prepare them that way. But while schools have been moving toward creating new expectations for student learning, schools of education have been lagging behind. With few exceptions, there are wide gaps between the emerging standards for what students ought to know and be able to do and the expectations for teachers.

One effort that could help link the two together is the move by the newly created National Board for Professional Teaching Standards to certify well-qualified teachers. A high-profile panel of teachers and public officials, the board is setting national standards for teaching excellence that are in many ways congruent with what schools are expecting students to know and be able to do. And the board is assessing teachers' abilities in new ways; in essence, it is creating a new way of knowing what teachers know. But the board's effort, while promising, is only part of the answer. To be sure, the board will set standards that all teachers can aim for. But it is intending to certify only highly qualified, experienced teachers. The rest will rely on state licensing standards. And because of the huge gulf that separates higher education and precollegiate education, those standards for the most part have not evolved to reflect the new expectations for students. As a result, schools of education will continue to turn out teachers prepared to teach in traditional ways. This must change.

As essential as the changes in teaching and teacher education are, they and any other changes in education can take place only with public support. As the Littleton experience indicates, public opposition can threaten any school reform. And even in the absence of opposition, a lack of support can hinder change, particularly a change that costs money to implement. But despite the well-documented problems in schools and the efforts of reformers, there does not appear to be a ground swell for dramatic change. Poll after poll has shown that, while the public is dissatisfied with the education system, people are pleased with their own schools. While this finding is not unique to education—similar dichotomies exist in public attitudes toward Congress and the medical profession, for example—it does suggest that many people would be reluctant to try a radical experiment in their own community or with their own children.

To generate public support, educators must make the case that the current expectations for student performance are inadequate. They must emphasize that a functioning democracy and an increasingly technological, high-skills economy demand graduates who can reason, solve problems, and communicate. They must show that we have learned that such skills are fundamental to learning. And they must explain that developing those abilities, and determining whether students have attained them, requires new methods of assessing student performance.

As educators since Horace Mann have known, developing students' knowledge and skills is the primary goal of schooling, and tests are a way of seeing how well schools have accomplished that objective. But as we have seen, tests have been more than that. They have also served both as the prime signal of what is valued and as a way of encouraging schools to focus on those valued outcomes. Educators and policy makers are now engaged in an extraordinary effort to redefine the outcomes they expect of students. As we have seen, they have a long way to go; and even if they succeed, they will have only begun the task of achieving their goals. But their work is a crucial step toward bringing about the level of achievement we should expect from every student. The road to the twenty-first century begins with a new way of knowing what young people know.

Glossary of Terms

Accountability: The process by which school districts and states attempt to ensure that schools and school systems meet their goals (such as the goal of improving the level of student performance). In the past two decades, states have tried a number of methods to hold schools accountable for raising student performance, including creating report cards to publicize student achievement, rewarding schools for superior performance with cash bonuses and freedom from regulation, and penalizing schools for declining performance.

Exhibition: An alternative form of assessment in which students orally, graphically, or in writing demonstrate the culmination of what they have learned, usually in a public way. The use of exhibitions as a requirement for graduation is a key principle of the Coalition of Essential Schools, a national network of reforming secondary schools.

High Stakes: Consequences attached to test performance. High stakes for students include the requirement that students pass tests in order to graduate from high school or to be eligible for special programs; for schools, they include rewards or sanctions based on test performance. Because those who are denied benefits based on test performance could challenge such decisions in court, high-stakes tests must meet technical standards for validity, reliability, and fairness. Low-stakes tests include those used by teachers to evaluate their own students' progress.

Inspectorate: A system, used in England and various other nations, that relies on independent observers to evaluate school performance. The observers monitor the teaching and learning in schools by observing classes and talking with teachers and administrators, and they then report their findings to the individual schools. A variation of the inspectorate system is being tested in New York State.

National Assessment of Educational Progress: A congressionally mandated, federally funded, federally operated project to measure student achievement in key subject areas. Created in 1969, NAEP tests about 100,000 students in grades four, eight, and twelve every two years in a range of subjects, including reading, writing, mathematics, science, U.S. history, and geography, and reports the results for the nation and major regions (and, since 1990, for participating states). The reports include data on instructional practices and student background, and they also offer information on trends in performance over time. The project is often called the "nation's report card."

National Assessment Governing Board: The independent body that sets policy for the National Assessment of Educational Progress. Created in 1988, the board consists of governors, state legislators, school board members, school administrators, teachers, curriculum specialists, testing experts, and members of the general public. The board ignited a major controversy by attempting to set standards for student performance on the assessment.

National Council on Education Standards and Testing: An independent panel created by Congress and the National Education Goals Panel in June 1991 to investigate the desirability and feasibility of national standards and assessments. Its 1992 report, *Raising Standards for American Education*, strongly endorsed national standards and a national assessment system linked to the standards. The council's proposal helped form the basis for the Goals 2000:

Educate America Act, signed into law by President Clinton in March 1994, which created a national body to certify voluntary national standards and state standards and assessments.

Opportunity to Learn: The extent to which students receive the type of instruction needed to answer test questions. Under the Goals 2000: Educate America Act, an independent body will set national standards for students' opportunity to learn.

Outcomes-Based Education: A system by which local school districts or states determine a set of outcomes for student performance, create assessments to measure attainment of the outcomes, and evaluate student school performance on the basis of the attainment of the outcomes. Outcomes-based systems stand in sharp contrast to traditional systems, in which school districts and states measure schools by "inputs," such as the number of courses taken or the pupil-teacher ratio. A major statewide attempt to create an outcomes-based system in Pennsylvania sparked a heated debate before the system was finally adopted. The controversy led other states and districts aiming toward similar goals to shun the use of the term "outcomes-based education."

Performance-Based Assessment: Tests that measure students' abilities to perform tasks, such as writing essays, completing science experiments, and solving mathematics problems, rather than choose answers from among a number of possible answers supplied.

Portfolio: An alternative form of assessment that evaluates student performance on the basis of work completed throughout the course of a year or series of years. Portfolio assessments often include opportunities for students (and others) to reflect on their work, including their growth over time.

Project: An alternative form of assessment that evaluates student performance on the basis of long-term, sustained work.

Reliability: The degree to which test results can be trusted. Reliability usually encompasses two elements: stability, or the consistency of administration of tests, and interrater reliability, or the consistency of judgment of student work. Psychometricians employ a number of statistical techniques to measure reliability and indicate the degree to which results can be reported with confidence in their accuracy.

Standards: Benchmarks against which students and schools measure their progress. Educators generally discuss three types of standards: content standards, which gauge curriculum and instruction; performance standards, which gauge the level of student achievement; and opportunity-to-learn standards, which gauge the capacity of schools to deliver the type of instruction tests measure. The idea of measuring student and school performance against standards represents a major departure for American education, which has tended to compare students and schools to one another. Under the Goals 2000: Educate America Act, a national council will for the first time certify voluntary national content and opportunity-to-learn standards.

Validity: The degree to which tests measure what they purport to measure and do not exert undue consequences on instruction. In order to evaluate validity, psychometricians study tests to determine if they are used appropriately.

Notes

Chapter 1

1. Quoted in A. T. Lockwood, "From Telling to Coaching," *Focus in Change* 3, no. 1 (Mar. 1991): 3.

2. R. Rothman, "Testing Shifts from Memorization to Investigation in Littleton, Colo.," *Education Week*, Apr. 22, 1992, pp. 1, 22–23.

3. Mark Twain Elementary School, "The Peak Performance Plan" (Littleton, Colo.: Mark Twain Elementary School, 1990).

4. Mark Twain Elementary School, "The Peak Performance Plan."

5. Rothman, "Testing Shifts from Memorization," p. 22.

6. H. O'Neil, *Final Report of Experimental Studies on Motivation and NAEP Test Performance* (Los Angeles: National Center for Research on Evaluation, Standards, and Student Testing, University of California, Los Angeles, 1992).

7. Rothman, "Testing Shifts from Memorization," p. 1.

8. Rothman, "Testing Shifts from Memorization," p. 22.

9. Rothman, "Testing Shifts from Memorization," p. 22.

10. Lockwood, "From Telling to Coaching," p. 4.

11. G. Wiggins, "Teaching to the (Authentic) Test," *Educational Leadership* 46, no. 7 (Apr. 1989): 42.

12.. Personal communication, Apr. 1992.

13. Lockwood, "From Telling to Coaching," p. 6.

14. "Littleton Report Card Obscures More Than It Illuminates," *Rocky Mountain News*, Feb. 23, 1992, p. 89.

15. Littleton High School, "The American School System Is Failing Us All" (Littleton, Colo.: Littleton High School, 1991).

16. Rothman, "Testing Shifts from Memorization," p. 22.

17. Source: Littleton High School.

18. Rothman, "Testing Shifts from Memorization," p. 23.

19. "Teacher Doubts Direction 2000 Effects," *Littleton Independent*, Apr. 2, 1992, pp. 9, 36.

20. Rothman, "Testing Shifts from Memorization," p. 23.

21. Quoted in J. Bingham, "School Board Election Could Become Referendum," *Denver Post*, Sept. 7, 1993, p. 3B.

22. D. P. Wolf, "Portfolio Assessment: Sampling Student Work," *Educational Leadership* 46, no. 7 (Apr. 1989): 35.

23. Personal communication, Oct. 1993.

24. Personal communication, Oct. 1993.

Chapter 2

1. Quoted in P. D. Chapman, *Schools as Sorters: Lewis M. Terman, Applied Psychology, and the Intelligence Testing Movement, 1890–1930* (New York: New York University Press, 1988), p. 33.

2. G. F. Madaus and others, *The Influence of Testing on Teaching Math and Science in Grades 4–12* (Chestnut Hill, Mass.: Center for the Study of Testing, Evaluation, and Educational Policy, Boston College, 1992). For the extent of teacher-made tests, see R. J. Stiggins, "Revitalizing Classroom Assessment," *Phi Delta Kappan* 69, no. 5, pp. 363–368.

3. L. B. Resnick and D. P. Resnick, "Standards, Curriculum, and Performance: A Historical and Comparative Perspective," *Educational Researcher* 16, no. 9: 13–20.

4. See Chapman, *Schools as Sorters*, and H. D. Corbett and B. L. Wilson, *Testing, Reform, and Rebellion* (Norwood, N.J.: Ablex, 1991), p. 18.

5. S. J. Gould, *The Mismeasure of Man* (New York: Norton, 1981), p. 195.

6. See Chapman, *Schools as Sorters*, pp. 146–170.

7. See A. E. Wise, *Legislated Learning* (Berkeley: University of California Press, 1979), pp. 12–26, for a more complete analysis of the accountability legislation.

8. W. Wirtz, *On Further Examination: Report of the Advisory Panel on the Scholastic Aptitude Test Decline* (New York: College Board, 1977), p. 1

9. National Commission on Excellence in Education, *A Nation At Risk* (Washington, D.C.: U.S. Government Printing Office, 1983), pp. 5, 27–28.

10. See E. L. Baker, "Mandated Tests: Educational Reform or Quality Indicator?" in *Test Policy and Test Performance: Education, Language, and Culture*, ed. B. R. Gifford (Boston: Kluwer, 1989). Also, see U.S. Congress, Office of Technology Assessment, *Testing in American Schools: Asking the Right Questions* (Washington, D.C.: U.S. Government Printing Office, 1992).

11. L. Alexander and H. T. James, *The Nation's Report Card: Improving the Assessment of Student Achievement* (Cambridge, Mass.: National Academy of Education, 1987).

12. See National Commission on Testing and Public Policy, *From Gatekeeper to Gateway: Transforming Testing in America* (Chestnut Hill, Mass.: Boston College, 1989); Madaus and others, *The Influence of Testing*; and U.S. General Accounting Office, *Student Testing: Current Extent and Expenditures, with Cost Estimates for a National Examination* (Washington, D.C.: U.S. Government Printing Office, 1993). Part of the confusion stems from the definition of *test*. The National Commission, for example, refers to each test in a battery as a separate test, while the Government Accounting Office does not.

13. Madaus and others, *The Influence of Testing*.

14. Quoted in G. F. Gaines and L. M. Cornett, *School*

Accountability Reports: Lessons Learned in S.R.E.B. States (Atlanta: Southern Regional Education Board, 1992, p. 16).

15. Madaus and others, *The Influence of Testing.*

16. S. M. Bennett and D. Carlson, "A Brief History of State Testing Policies in California," in *State Educational Testing Policies* (Washington, D.C.: Office of Technology Assessment, 1986, p.169).

Chapter 3

1. J. J. Cannell, *Nationally Normed Elementary Achievement Testing in America's Public Schools: How All Fifty States Are Above the National Average* (Daniels, W.Va.: Friends for Education, 1987); Cineol updated his survey two years later, after moving to New Mexico to study psychiatry. See J. J. Cannell, *How Public Educators Cheat on Standardized Achievement Tests* (Albuquerque, N.M.: Friends for Education, 1989).

2. See S. J. Gould, *The Mismeasure of Man* (New York: Norton), 1981.

3. L. Salmon-Cox, "Teachers and Standardized Achievement Tests: What's Really Happening," *Phi Delta Kappan* 62, no. 9: 631–634. Also see D. Dorr-Bremme and J. Herman, *Assessing Student Achievement: A Profile of Classroom Practices* (Los Angeles: Center for the Study of Evaluation, University of California, Los Angeles, 1986).

4. R. L. Linn, M. E. Graue, and N. M. Sanders, *Comparing State and District Test Results to National Norms: Interpretations of Scoring "Above the National Average,"* Technical Report (Boulder: Center for Research on Evaluation, Standards, and Student Testing, University of Colorado, 1989).

5. I.V.S. Mullis and others, *Trends in Academic Progress* (Washington, D.C.: U.S. Government Printing Office, 1991).

6. See Cannell, *How Public Educators Cheat;* G. Putka, "Classroom Scandal: Cheaters in Schools May Not Be Students

But Their Teachers," *Wall Street Journal*, Nov. 2, 1989, p. A1; E. Woo, "40 Grade Schools Cheated on Skill Tests, State Finds," *Los Angeles Times*, Sept. 1, 1988, p. 1; G. Putka, "Blackboard Jungle: A Cheating Epidemic at a Top High School Teaches Sad Lessons," *Wall Street Journal*, June 29, 1992, p. A1.

7. A. McGill-Franzen and R. L. Allington, "Flunk 'em or Get Them Classified: The Contamination of Primary Grade Accountability Data," *Educational Researcher* 22, no. 1 (Jan./Feb. 1993): 19–22.

8. L. A. Shepard, "Inflated Test Score Gains: Is It Old Norms or Teaching to the Test?" (paper presented at the annual meeting of the American Educational Research Association, San Francisco, 1989).

9. H. D. Corbett and B. L. Wilson, *Testing, Reform, and Rebellion* (Norwood, N.J.: Ablex, 1991), p. 78. Also see T. H. Haladyna, S. B. Nolen, and N. S. Haas, "Raising Standardized Test Scores and the Origins of Test Score Pollution," *Educational Researcher* 20, no. 5 (June/July 1991): 2–7.

10. See Shepard, "Inflated Test Score Gains," p. 15.

11. See G. F. Madaus and others, *The Influence of Testing on Teaching Math and Science in Grades 4–12* (Chestnut Hill, Mass.: Center for the Study of Testing, Evaluation, and Educational Policy, Boston College, 1992); and J. L. Herman and S. Golan, "The Effects of Standardized Testing on Teaching and Schools," *Educational Measurement: Issues and Practice*, Winter 1993, pp. 20–25.

12. Corbett and Wilson, *Testing, Reform, and Rebellion*, p. 102.

13. L. Cronbach, "Evaluation of Course Improvement," *Teachers College Record* 64 (1963): 672–683.

14. See Herman and Golan, "The Effects of Standardized Testing."

15. D. M. Koretz, R. L. Linn, S. B. Dunbar, and L. A. Shepard, "The Effects of High-Stakes Testing on Achievement: Pre-

liminary Findings About Generalization Across Tests" (paper presented at the annual meeting of the American Educational Research Association, Chicago, Apr. 1991).

16. National Council of Teachers of Mathematics, *Curriculum and Evaluation Standards for School Mathematics* (Reston, Va.: National Council of Teachers of Mathematics, 1989).

17. Madaus and others, *The Influence of Testing*.

18. Mullis and others, *Trends in Academic Progress*.

19. N. Frederiksen, "The Real Test Bias: Influences of Testing on Teaching and Learning," *American Psychologist* 39, no. 1 (Mar. 1984): 193–202.

20. For research on cognitive science and education, see L. B. Resnick, "Learning In School and Out," *Educational Researcher*, 16, no. 9, pp. 13–19; L. B. Resnick and L. Klopfer, eds., *Toward the Thinking Curriculum: Current Cognitive Research* (Alexandria, Va.: Association for Supervision and Curriculum Development, 1989); and J. T. Bruer, *Schools for Thought: A Science of Learning in the Classroom* (Cambridge, Mass.: MIT Press, 1993).

21. H. Gardner, *The Unschooled Mind: How Children Think and How Schools Should Teach* (New York: Basic Books, 1991).

22. D. N. Perkins, "Pedagogy of Understanding" (paper presented at the annual meeting of the American Educational Research Association, Atlanta, Apr. 1993).

23. L. B. Resnick and D. P. Resnick, "Assessing the Thinking Curriculum: New Tools for Educational Reform," in *Changing Assessments: Alternative Views of Aptitude, Achievement, and Instruction*, ed B. R. Gifford and M. C. O'Connor (Boston: Kluwer, 1992).

24. See H. Gardner, *Frames of Mind* (New York: Basic Books, 1983); R. J. Sternberg, *Beyond IQ: A Triarchic Theory of Human Intelligence* (Cambridge, Mass.: Cambridge University Press, 1985).

25. Resnick and Resnick, "Assessing the Thinking Curriculum," p. 59.

26. T. R. Sizer, *Horace's School* (Boston: Houghton Mifflin, 1992), pp. 25–26.

Chapter 4

1. R. P. Mills, "Portfolios Capture Rich Array of Student Performance," *School Administrator* 46, no. 11 (Dec. 1989): 10.

2. U.S. Congress, Office of Technology Assessment, *Testing in American Schools: Asking the Right Questions* (Washington, D.C.: U.S. Government Printing Office, 1992), p. 203.

3. Vermont Department of Education, *Looking Beyond "the Answer": The Report of Vermont's Mathematics Portfolio Assessment Program* (Montpelier: Vermont Department of Education, 1991).

4. D. Koretz, B. Stecher, and E. Deibert, *The Vermont Portfolio Assessment Program: Interim Report on Implementation and Impact, 1991–92 School Year* (Los Angeles: National Center for Research on Evaluation, Standards, and Student Testing, University of California, Los Angeles, 1992).

5. California Assessment Program, *A Sampler of English–Language Arts Assessment* (Sacramento: California Department of Education, 1992), p. 2.

6. Quoted in L. Olson, "Off and Running," in *From Risk to Renewal: Charting a Course for Reform*, ed. Editors of *Education Week* (Washington, D.C.: Editorial Projects in Education, 1993, p. 169).

7. Kentucky Department of Education, *Quick Guide to Student Assessment in Kentucky* (Frankfort, Ky.: Kentucky Department of Education, n.d.).

8. Personal communication, Sept. 1992.

9. "State Reports Test Results for 4th, 8th, and 12th

Graders" (press release, Kentucky Department of Education, Sept. 30, 1993).

Chapter 5

1. Congress in 1994 added two additional goals: by the year 2000, members of the nation's teaching force will have access to programs for the continued improvement of their professional skills and the opportunity to acquire the knowledge and skills needed to instruct and prepare all U.S. students for the next century; and every school will promote partnerships that will increase parental involvement and participation in promoting the social, emotional, and academic growth of children.

2. R. Rothman, "2 Groups Laying Plans to Develop National Exams," *Education Week*, Sept. 26, 1990, pp. 1, 14.

3. For mathematics results, see C. C. McKnight and others, *The Underachieving Curriculum* (Champaign, Ill.: Stipes, 1987); and A. E. LaPointe, J. M. Askew, and N. A. Mead, *Learning Mathematics* (Princeton, N.J.: Educational Testing Service, 1992). For science results, see International Association for the Evaluation of Educational Achievement, *Science Achievement in Seventeen Countries: A Preliminary Report* (Oxford: Pergamon Press, 1988); and A. E. LaPointe, J. M. Askew, and N. A. Mead, *Learning Science* (Princeton, N.J.: Educational Testing Service, 1992). For reading literacy, see W. B. Elley, *How in the World Do Students Read?* (Hamburg, Germany: International Association for the Evaluation of Educational Achievement, 1992).

4. For Rickover's views, see H. Rickover, *Swiss Schools and Ours: Why Theirs Are Better* (Boston: Little, Brown, 1962); and H. Rickover, *American Education: A National Failure* (New York: Dutton, 1963).

5. National Endowment for the Humanities, *National Tests: What Other Countries Expect Their Students to Know*

(Washington, D.C.: National Endowment for the Humanities, 1991), p. 2.

6. National Council of Teachers of Mathematics, *Curriculum and Evaluation Standards for School Mathematics* (Reston, Va.: National Council of Teachers of Mathematics, 1989).

7. American Association for the Advancement of Science, *Science for All Americans* (Washington, D.C.: American Association for the Advancement of Science, 1989).

8. See W. J. Bennett, *James Madison High School: A Curriculum for American Students* (Washington, D.C.: U.S. Department of Education, 1987); E. D. Hirsch, *Cultural Literacy: What Every American Needs to Know* (Boston: Houghton Mifflin, 1987).

9. S. M. Elam and A. M. Gallup, "The 21st Annual Gallup Poll of the Public's Attitudes Toward the Public Schools," *Phi Delta Kappan* 71, no. 1 (Sept. 1989): 41–56.

10. Quoted in Rothman, "2 Groups Laying Plans," p. 1.

11. U.S. Department of Education, *America 2000: An Education Strategy* (Washington, D.C.: U.S. Department of Education, 1991).

12. Commission on the Skills of the American Workforce, *America's Choice: High Skills or Low Wages?* (Rochester, N.Y.: National Center on Education and the Economy, 1990).

13. Quoted in Rothman, "2 Groups Laying Plans," p. 14.

14. National Council on Education Standards and Testing, *Raising Standards for American Education* (Washington, D.C.: National Council on Education Standards and Testing, 1992).

15. Quoted in R. Rothman, "Council Calls for a New System of Standards, Tests," *Education Week*, Jan. 29, 1992, pp. 1, 30.

16. Personal communication, Jan. 1992.

17. Testimony before the House Education and Labor Subcommittee on Elementary, Secondary, and Vocational Education, Feb. 19, 1992.

18. U.S. Congress, Office of Technology Assessment, *Testing in American Schools: Asking the Right Questions* (Washington, D.C.: U.S. Government Printing Office, 1992), p. 30.

19. U.S. Congress, Office of Technology Assessment, *Testing in American Schools*, p. 136.

20. Personal communication, Feb. 1992.

Chapter 6

1. Pennsylvania Department of Education, "Rules and Regulations," Title 22, Chapter 5, *Pennsylvania Bulletin* 23, no. 30 (July 24, 1993): 3549–3565.

2. Personal communication, Mar. 1992.

3. Quoted in U.S. Congress, Office of Technology Assessment, *Testing in American Schools: Asking the Right Questions* (Washington, D.C.: U.S. Government Printing Office, 1992), p. 246.

4. "Another Educational Experiment: Restructuring at Heritage" (unpublished flyer, June 2, 1993).

5. R. L. Linn, E. L. Baker, and S. B. Dunbar, *Complex, Performance-Based Assessment and Validation Criteria*, Technical Report (Los Angeles: Center for Research on Evaluation, Standards, and Student Testing, University of California, Los Angeles, 1991).

6. N. Webb, *Collaborative Group Versus Individual Assessment in Mathematics*, Technical Report (Los Angeles: Center for Research on Evaluation, Standards, and Student Testing, University of California, Los Angeles, 1993).

7. R. J. Shavelson, X. Gao, and G. P. Baxter, *Sampling Variability of Performance Assessments*, Technical Report (Los Angeles: Center for Research on Evaluation, Standards, and Student Testing, University of California, Los Angeles, 1993).

8. Personal communication, Sept. 1993.

9. D. Koretz and others, *The Reliability of Scores from the 1992 Vermont Portfolio Assessment Program*, Technical Report

(Los Angeles: Center for Research on Evaluation, Standards, and Student Testing, University of California, Los Angeles, 1993).

10. J. A. Dossey, I.V.S. Mullis, and C. O. Jones, *Can Students Do Mathematical Problem Solving?* (Washington, D.C.: National Center for Education Statistics, 1993).

11. R. Rothman, "NAEP to Create Three Standards for Performance," *Education Week*, May 23, 1990, p. 1.

12. U.S. General Accounting Office, *Educational Achievement Standards: NAGB's Approach Yields Misleading Interpretations* (Washington, D.C.: U.S. General Accounting Office, 1993); National Academy of Education, *Setting Performance Standards for Student Achievement* (Stanford, Calif.: National Academy of Education, 1993).

13. U.S. Congress, Office of Technology Assessment, *Testing in American Schools*, pp. 28–29.

14. U.S. General Accounting Office, *Student Testing: Current Extent and Expenditures, with Cost Estimates for a National Examination* (Washington, D.C.: U.S. Government Printing Office, 1993).

15. R. Rothman, "New Tests Based on Performance Raise Questions," *Education Week*, Sept. 12, 1990, p. 10.

Chapter 7

1. J. Kozol, *Savage Inequalities: Children in America's Schools* (New York: Crown, 1991).

2. C. C. McKnight and others, *The Underachieving Curriculum* (Champaign, Ill.: Stipes, 1987).

3. F. I. Stevens, *Opportunity to Learn: Issues of Equity for Poor and Minority Students* (Washington, D.C.: National Center for Education Statistics, 1993).

4. L. Darling-Hammond, *Standards of Practice for Learner-Centered Schools* (New York: National Center for Restructuring Education, Schools, and Teaching, 1992); J. O'Day and M. S.

Smith, "Systemic School Reform and Educational Opportunity," in *Designing Coherent Education Policy: Improving the System*, ed. S. Fuhrman (San Francisco: Jossey-Bass, 1993).

5. D. K. Cohen, "Revolution in One Classroom (or Then Again, Was It?)," *American Educator* 15, no. 2 (Fall 1991): pp. 16–23, 44–48.

Index

Science: and curriculum reform, 118; performance-based assessments in, 97, 155–156
Scores, national averages, 40, 55–56, 64, 113, 177
Score raising: versus achievement, 129; effect on student learning, 62; as unethical practice, 56–58
Scoring: machine, development of, 38; norm-referenced, 53–58; of portfolios, 82, 159; by private firms, 105; reliability, 158–159; subjectivity, 148–149; teacher involvement in, 100–101, 148–149; and "teaching to the test," 58–65; training for, 100, 159
Scoring guides (rubrics), 13
Secrecy, traditional testing, 5, 54
Security, test, 56
Self-assessment, 73
Shanker, A., 112, 115–116, 120
Shavelson, R. J., 155–156
Shepard, L. A., 58–59, 60, 62
Sizer, T. R., 74
Smith, L., 26
Smith, M. S., 179–180
Social studies assessment, 97–98; and curriculum reform, 119
South Carolina: deregulation program, 48; school takeover approach, 48
Standards: implied, 112–113; student awareness of, 13–16, 29–30
Standards-setting, 192; attempt by National Assessment Governing Board, 164–167; New Standards Project, 79, 123–127, 139, 177–178; public process of, 73; by test publishers, 55
State-by-state testing comparisons, 42
State ranking, 44–46
Statewide programs, 32, 38, 41, 77–80; comparisons of, 42; portfolio, 80–89. *See also specific state*
Stecher, B., 88
Stein, R., 28
Sternberg, R. J., 69–70
Stevens, F. I., 177
Stiggins, R. J., 35
Systemwide testing, time investment of, 43

T

Teachers' goals, and test content, 63–64
Teachers as coaches, 6, 14

Teaching to the test: and disadvantaged and minority students, 60, 61–62; and scoring, 58–65
Technical obstacles, 149–151
Test of Essential Learning and Literacy Skills (TELLS), 142–143
Test publishers: development of alternative testing, 92; norm-setting, 55
Testing: and accountability, 39–40; and concern with student achievement, 40; history and development of, 33–34, 36–38; as management tool, 36; second wave, 1960s to present, 38–43
Textbooks: criticism of, 5; and implied national standards, 112–113; quality of, 129
"Thinking curriculum," 19, 65–68
Thinking–skills assessment, 10–11
Thorndike, E. L., 37
Time investment, 43, 169–170
"Triarchic" theory of intelligence, 69–70
Turner, K., 9, 156

U

Unschooled Mind, The, 67

V

Validity issue, 17, 152–156, 192
Vermont, portfolio testing program in, 80–89, 158–160; effectiveness evaluation, 87–88; implementation time, 87
Vision, school, 8, 19–20

W

Webb, N., 154, 156
Weber, S., 148–149
Westerberg, T., 20
Wiggins, G., 15, 73, 171
Wilson, B. L., 37, 59, 60–61
Wilson, P., 90, 91, 102
Wirtz, W., 40
Wise, A. E., 39
Wolf, D. P., 27
Writing assessment. *See* Reading and writing assessment
Writing portfolios, 81–82

Y

Yoshida, C., 29
Young, L., 24